THE

BOURNE SOCIETY

Village Histories

3. SANDERSTEAD

(including Selsdon)

Editor: Joy Gadsby

Series Editors - Roger Packham & Gwyneth Fookes

ISBN 0 900992 44 1

Acknowledgements

This history of Sanderstead has been compiled very much as a team effort, all the members of which have given generously of their time in researching, recording and reviewing the contents. They have worked together for five years with patience, enthusiasm and forbearance, making the editor's job a pleasure to perform. Their names are to be found under the appropriate chapters, but their contribution far exceeds any specific authorship.

We are also greatly indebted to many other members of the Bourne Society, local residents, the staff of the Croydon Local Studies and Sanderstead libraries and the various Public Record and newspaper offices that we have consulted; we have also gleaned a great deal of information from earlier writers of local history.

Above all, thanks go to the editors of the Village History Series, Gwyneth Fookes and Roger Packham, and to Dr. Robert Warner for help with desk-top publishing, without whose help, encouragement and final coercion this book would never have been published.

JMG

Cover photograph:

Sanderstead Today

A photograph looking across Sanderstead Pond, at the top of Sanderstead Hill, towards All Saints' Church.

CONTENTS

Introduction --- 1

1   Foundations   by Joy Gadsby ----------------------------- 3

2   Early Sanderstead & the Domesday Record   by Joy Gadsby ----------------------------- 5

3   Life in the Manor   by Joy Gadsby & Bob Adams --------------- 13

4   Tudor Times   by Joy Gadsby & Francis Davison --------- 17

5   Regicide, Civil War and the Aftermath   by Joy Gadsby & Bob Adams --------------- 23

6   19th Century – An Estate Village   by Bob Adams ----------------------------- 33

7   Early Expansion   by Bob Adams, Vernon Briggs & Ted Frith - 45

8   The Great War 1914 – 1918   by Roger Packham ------------------------- 51

9   The Old Order Changes – between the wars   by Joy Gadsby ----------------------------- 59

10 World War II 1939 – 1945   by Joy Gadsby ----------------------------- 63

11 The Last Fifty Years   by Joy Gadsby ----------------------------- 67

12 Education Then and Now   by Francis Davison ----------------------- 71

13 Communications – Moving onto
    the Fast Track   byTerry Carroll -------------------------- 81

14 From Village Store to Supermarket   by Francis Davison ----------------------- 95

15 Churches and Chapels   by Margaret Isted Osborn ---------------- 107

16 Aspects of Social Life   by Vernon Briggs, Olive Carroll, Ted Frith,
                                                  Joy Gadsby & J. Hewett-Hicks ------------ 115

17 The Natural World around Us   by Joy Gadsby --------------------------- 125

18 People Past and Present   by all contributors --------------------- 135

19 A-Z of Road Names   by Vernon Briggs ------------------------ 143

20 A History of Selsdon   by Ted Frith ---------------------------- 153

21 Chronology   by Joy Gadsby --------------------------- 167

LIST OF ILLUSTRATIONS

Page No.

Forethought

VIII   An oak tree on Sanderstead Hill – painting by J.B. James

2   Map of the Villages of the Bourne Area

Chapter 1 Foundations

3   Fossil sea urchin in flint found in Blackheath Pebble Beds

4   Map of geology of Sanderstead and Selsdon

4   Map of the contours of Sanderstead and Selsdon

Chapter 2 Early Sanderstead and the Domesday Record

5   Prehistoric finds in Sanderstead and Selsdon

6   Broken mesolithic flint axe or pick found at Purley Downs Road

6   Drawings of dandelion and ramsons

8   Roman pot

8   Romano-British Child's Feeding Bottle

8   Children from Atwood School – each child is standing in an excavated Romano-British post hole

9   Aelderman Alfred's Will

10   Map Showing link between Sanderstead, the sub-manor of Langhurst and Lingfield

Chapter 3 Life in the Manor

14   Wall paintings *in situ*

14   14th century wall paintings representing St. Edmund the Martyr, King of East Anglia and St. Edmund, Archbishop of Canterbury

14   Piscina from All Saints' Church

15   Main door of All Saints' Church

16   Stone Figure in the nave, thought to represent one of the 13th century masons

16   Figure of Queen from South Porch

Chapter 4 Tudor Times

18   Brass of John & Dyones Atwood

18   Brass of seven sons and three daughters of Nicholas Atwood

19   Memorial to John Ownstead

20   'The White House' – on record at least from the 14th century

21   An interior of 'The White House' from an article in *Ideal Home*, August 1937

22   Conjectural map of Sanderstead in Queen Elizabeth's Reign

Chapter 5 Regicide, Civil War and its Aftermath

23   The Armorial Achievement of Harman Atwood

24   Suggested line of succession of the Atwood family from the 16th to 18th centuries

25   'Sanderstead Court' built by Harman Atwood in 1676

26   Sketchline of the descent of the Sanderstead Estate from Atwood through Wigsell to Arkwright 18th-20th centuries

27   Tomb of Maria Audley, wife of Major Lewis Audley, who died in 1655

27   The George Mellish memorial dated 1693

27   Detail from the George Mellish memorial

29   The Forge, which dates from the 18th century

29   Sanderstead Rectory, believed to have been built by Olive Atwood, painted by Hassell *c.*1825

29   'Purley Bury House', built in the 17th century

31   The section of Rocque Map, 1764, which covers Sanderstead

Chapter 6 19th Century – Estate Village

32   Map of Sanderstead in 1843 from the plan annexed to the tithe award

34   Purley Downs near Croydon, 1885, a painting by T. Whittle

35   Purley Oaks, pre 1925, a painting by Ethel Hall

35   A trefoil window in All Saints' Church, showing the arms of the Diocese of Winchester, Wigsell and Courtney

37   Thought to be Borough Farm, *c.*1880

37   Old Fox path *c.*1900

41   The farmhouses of Sanderstead and Selsdon in 1910

41   Fox Farm, 1997

43   Sanderstead Road, a painting by J.B. James

Chapter 7 Early Expansion

46   The Poor Law Station in Sanderstead Road, photographed in 1998

47   Housing developed soon after the arrival of the railway – Mayfield Road

47   The same view in 1997

49   Pumping water outside the village school, 1906

50   1-3 Penwortham Road, photographed in 1998

Page No.

Chapter 8 The Great War 1914 - 1918

51 The War Memorial

52 Boy Scouts outside the school in 1914 – Scouts contributed greatly to the war effort

54 Sanderstead Memorial Hall, photographed in 1997

57 1919 Peace celebrations outside the village school

Chapter 9 The Old Order Changes – Between the Wars

58 The fire station, opened in 1936

58 Phoenix House built on the site of the fire station, 1998

60 Telephone exchange in Church Way, built in 1931

61 The fire brigade in 1936

Chapter 10 World War II 1939 -1945

62 A wartime wedding, 1939

64 Menu for the Platoon dinner, 1944

66 East window in All Saints' Church, using surviving glass after bomb damage

Chapter 11 The Last Fifty Years

67 The traffic island at the top of Sanderstead Hill, constructed in the 1970s

68 Rectory Court built on the site of the old rectory, post 1945, photo 1997

69 Photograph of Cedar Court taken from the church roof, built in the 1970s

Chapter 12 Education Then and Now

70 Drawing of the village school in 1831

72 The village school built 1875, photo *c.*1907

73 *Right* – Mrs. Small, school head. *Left* – Mrs. Cowdrey and 'Gyp'. *c.*1916

74 The Upper School, 1920

76 Map showing development of Schools

78 St. Anne's College, photographed pre-war

80 Little Heath School 1929

Chapter 13 Communications – Moving onto the Fast Track

82 Mrs. Cowdrey and Mrs. Small in the cab from the station, pre-1921

85 Staff at Purley Oaks Station early 20th century

85 The last train on the Woodside-Sanderstead line 1983

86 The last steam train at Sanderstead Station – engine No. 34108 *Wincanton*, 1967

Page No.

87	Map showing railway and bus routes in 1997
90	Tilling bus on Sanderstead Hill *c.*1921
90	The same view in 1998 with service No. 403
92	Advertisement for the Great Air Display in 1935
93	An air ambulance on Sanderstead recreation ground, 1994

Chapter 14 From Village Store to Supermarket

95	The village shop *c.*1896 with the Frosel family
97	Station Parade, Sanderstead Road, *c.*1930
97	The same view in 1997
99	Hubbard & Nash's shop in Addington Road *c.*1931
100	Purley Oaks Parade in 1998
101	Cranleigh Parade, Limpsfield Road, before 1962
101	From Cranleigh Parade towards the school, on a December day in the 1980s
102	Hamsey Green Parade – from an old postcard (1936)
104	Map showing development of shopping areas in Sanderstead and Selsdon
106	Postmarks from 1845

Chapter 15 Churches and Chapels

107	St. Gertrude's Church, built 1906, photographed in 1997
108	Map of places of worship
109	Interior of St. Gertrude's Church, from an old postcard
109	Bourne Society Plaque at St. Anne's College
110	St. Mary's Church, Beech Avenue/Purley Oaks Road, photographed in 1997
111	Sanderstead Congregational Church Ladies' Committee, May 1933
112	All Saints' Church choir, 1950
112	Raising funds to extend All Saints' Church to celebrate the 750th anniversary, 1980
113	Bishop Howard Tripp unveiling the Bourne Society plaque
114	St. Antony's Church, Hamsey Green, with the Revd. David Haywood 1998

Chapter 16 Aspects of Social Life

115	Walkers (and their canine companions) enjoying a stroll along the main ride in King's Wood, 1997
117	Sanderstead Cricketers, 1981
117	Purley Downs Golf Course, photographed in 1998
118	Entrance to Selsdon Park Golf Club – from an old postcard
120	Sanderstead Dramatic Club Junior Section

Page No.

121   Mrs. Cecilia Muckelroy planting a tree in the Wettern Tree Garden

123   Sea Rangers at Camp, 1946

123   Cubs, Scouts, Brownies and Guides with the Revd. Howard Rose in the Rectory garden

124   A leisure centre in the future now that we have acquired a pub?

Chapter 17 The Natural World Around Us

126   The sinuous boundary of King's Wood, which also forms the parish boundary, photographed in 1998

126   A Bourne Society group studies an interesting find in King's Wood, 1986

127   Coombe Wood on the summit of Riddlesdown, c.1900, painting by Ethel Hall

128   Sanderstead Village pond by the Gruffy

130   Meadow saxifrage

130   A Bank vole's hole in the churchyard

116   Bee orchids suddenly appeared in a local field

132   Adders and grass snakes escaping the drought in a swimming pool in Purley Downs Road, 1975

132   The 'Fox Box' at Sanderstead Library

133   Young nature detectives at work, c.1994

Chapter 18 People Past and Present

135   A Mellish coat of arms

136   Sanderstead Mounted Patrol Station, 1933

137   Memorial to Henrietta Smith, who left 111 direct surviving descendants

137   Memorial to Oswald Smith and Frances Dora

137   The Smith family vault in All Saints' Churchyard

138   Tom Sherlock

138   Malcolm G. Sharpe

140   Memorial to Betty Margaret Zeal in All Saints' Churchyard

140   Ruth Ellis

141   Mrs. Martha Rosier

141   George Gadsby

141   Miss Phyllis Revell

Chapter 19 An A-Z of Road Names

142   The growth of Sanderstead in over a century – 1875-1988

143   Addington Road, Sanderstead, c.1935

144   Beech Avenue – from an old postcard. St. Anne's College in the background

145   Brambledown Road

Page No.

146   Florence Road today (1998)

147   A house with family group. Florence Road. *c*.1908

147   Glebe Hyrst

133   Limpsfield Road, *c*.1924. Beechview Cottages (18th century) in the foreground

149   Mitchley Hill, photgraphed in 1998

150   Purley Downs Road, with the lodge to 'Purley Bury House' in the foreground. From an old postcard

151   Riddlesdown Road, where it opens out onto the Corportion of London's Riddlesdown. 1998

Chapter 20 A History of Selsdon

154   Extract of Archbishop Morton's Terrier, 1492

156   Kingswood Lodge, the oldest building in Selsdon, undergoing restoration in 1998

156   Selsdon Park, painting by Hassell, 1820

157   Old Farleigh Road, looking north-west from entrance to Selsdon Woods. *c*.1905

157   Addington Road cottages *c*.1906

160   The Costain bus *c*.1929

162   A Bren gun carrier, which had seen service in Norway, giving rides to children in Addington Road, 29th November 1941

163   'Selsdon Smiles' started in January 1947 with a dig at the bus service

166   A Costain House in 1928

Chapter 21 Chronology

171   Weathervane atop the wooden shingled spire of All Saints'

FORETHOUGHT

'No—one is a child of today;
You are the child of a thousand years.
Deep through layer after layer
The roots go down.'

Knut Hauge
(Norwegian poet 1911 – 1993)

These words are as true of a village as they are of a family. We hope, through the pages that follow, to show you how past peoples and events have influenced and shaped the Sanderstead of today.

Introduction

THE BOURNE SOCIETY six years ago set itself the task of publishing a substantial general history of each of the several parishes within its study area - this volume is the third. The first volume on Purley was produced in autumn 1996 and was received with great enthusiasm, to such an extent that ten excerpts were published in *The Coulsdon & Purley Advertiser* and the first print run was sold out just after Christmas the same year. The second volume, on Caterham, followed in autumn 1997, and received a similarly enthusiastic welcome. Once again a number of excerpts were published in *The Caterham Advertiser*. If the project reaches its ultimate goal, there will be thirteen volumes, that is ten beyond the current volume - Chaldon, Chelsham, Chipstead, Coulsdon, Farleigh, Godstone, Kenley, Warlingham, Whyteleafe and Woldingham.

The research team formed for each of the proposed books will almost certainly include some members with considerable experience in researching and publishing their particular subject. Others will be embarking on research for the first time and hopefully will find that their subject expands and becomes more intriguing the more they explore. The Sanderstead team has worked very enthusiastically and has embarked on projects far beyond the call of the chapters in this book. With Joy Gadsby's guidance they have met frequently and enjoyed sharing their accumulating knowledge. It has been a pleasure to join them on these occasions.

This history of Sanderstead does not claim to be the definitive history and it is hoped that it will serve to stimulate the interest of residents in their locality and some may be sufficiently enthused to become involved themselves in their local history. The editors would be very pleased to hear from readers who have information and/or illustrations that give further insight into the people and events detailed in the following pages.

Roger Packham
Gwyneth Fookes

May 1998

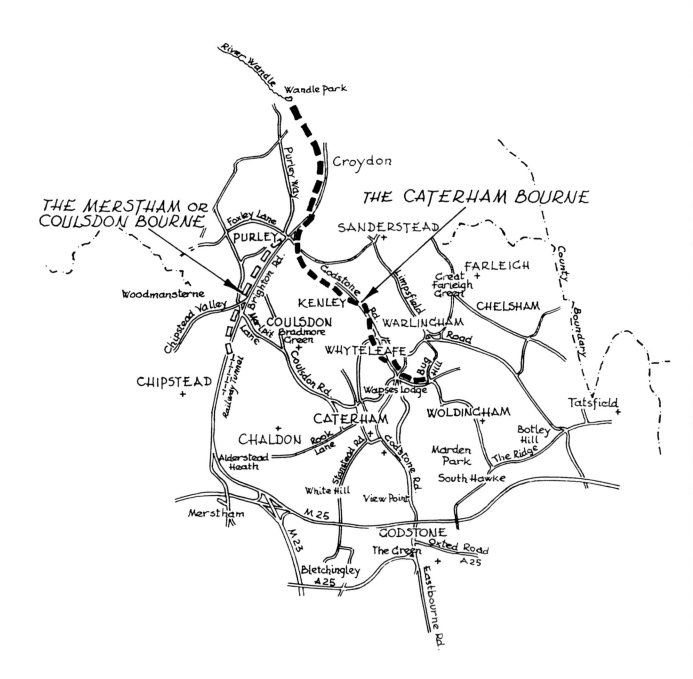

The Bourne Society Area

Chapter 1

Foundations

by Joy Gadsby

Standing at a high vantage point in the centre of Sanderstead, 181.9 metres (596 feet) above sea-level, it is difficult to imagine that this whole area was once under the sea; and yet that is where the history of Sanderstead can rightly be said to have begun.

The oldest part of the village is situated on the North Downs some three miles south-east of Croydon. The underlying rock is chalk, almost pure calcium carbonate, formed under warm shallow seas about 100 million years ago in the period known geologically as the Cretaceous. Associated with the chalk are bands of flints – a form of silica – and capping the chalk to the south of the village is a variable deposit of clay-with-flints. In places this has been found to be as much as six metres thick; elsewhere it is much thinner.

At the centre of the village, on the ridge running eastwards towards Addington, the chalk is overlain by sand, forming part of a more recent series of marine deposits known as the Thanet beds. It is from this sandy layer at its heart that the village takes its name. At the highest points are deposits of Blackheath pebbles.

Undisputed evidence of Sanderstead's undersea origins has been found in fossils within the chalk and flints, as for example a sea urchin and sponge that were found in King's Wood in September 1986.

The modern parish of Sanderstead has developed along a prehistoric trackway. The geology of the area – a hilltop site rich in light workable sandy soils, flint, clay, and the possibility of ponding and storing water despite the absence of a river or stream, provided all the essential ingredients for early human settlement. As will be seen from the following chapters, such settlement began in prehistoric times and has continued virtually unbroken right up to the present day.

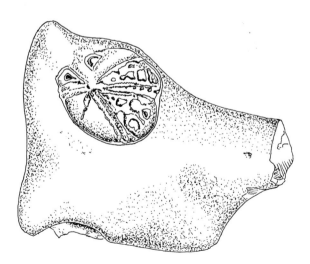

Fossil of Sea Urchin (*Micraster sp.*) found in a flint in Blackheath Pebble

SOURCES
British Geological Survey - East Surrey.

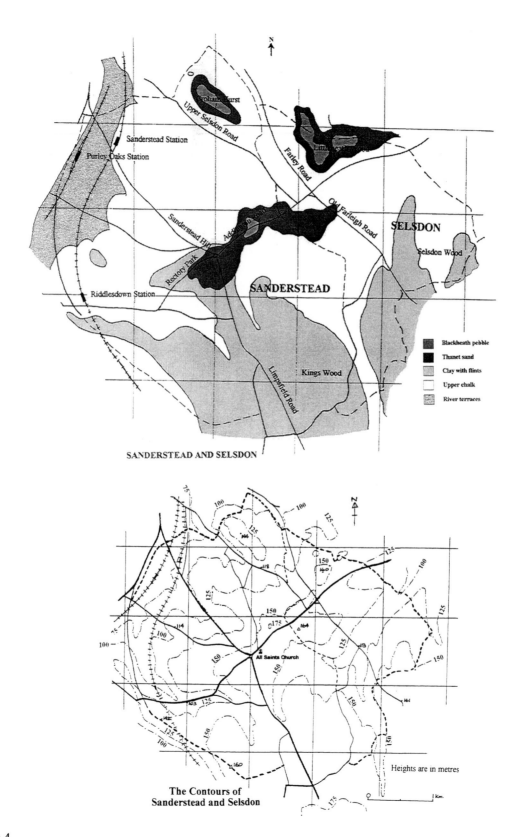

SANDERSTEAD AND SELSDON

Legend:
- Blackheath pebble
- Thanet sand
- Clay with flints
- Upper chalk
- River terraces

The Contours of
Sanderstead and Selsdon

Heights are in metres

Chapter 2

Early Sanderstead and the Domesday Record

by Joy Gadsby

Sanderstead was given its name by the Anglo-Saxons, who recognised its geological significance as a 'sandy place', but the origins of settlement go back into prehistory. The first people for whom we have evidence in Sanderstead were nomadic hunter-gatherers of the Mesolithic Period (or Middle Stone Age), who crossed the land bridge which then joined Britain to the rest of Europe and foraged along the high ground of south-east England, including the North Downs. They were probably here from about 7000 BC and have left signs of their presence in the form of simple but effective flint tools, for which they found a rich resource in the clay-with-flints capping that covers much of the chalk.

We know from archaeological finds in other parts of Britain that our Mesolithic forefathers probably lived in 'tents' made from timber or bone stakes covered with animal skins and weighted down with stones. Such dwellings would have been warm and weatherproof and fairly quickly constructed but the timber would have had to be cut using flint axes and moved into place by manpower, possibly using ropes made from plant materials or wooden rollers. The wheel had not yet been introduced. The efficiency and speed with which trees can be felled with a flint axe has been amply demonstrated in recent years by archaeologists. Experiments in Denmark have shown that it takes just 30 minutes to fell a mature Birch.

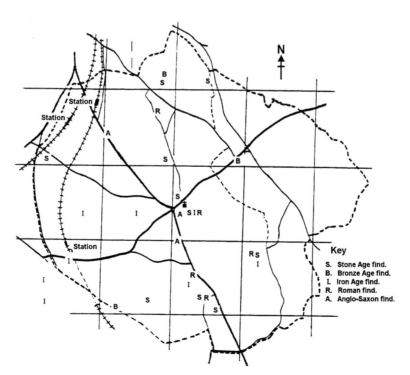

Key
S. Stone Age find.
B. Bronze Age find.
I. Iron Age find.
R. Roman find.
A. Anglo-Saxon find.

PREHISTORIC, ROMAN & ANGLO-SAXON FINDS

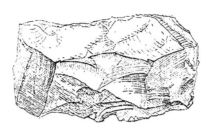

The butt end, measuring 8.5 x 5 x 3 cm, of a broken mesolithic flint axe or pick found at Purley Downs Road in 1948.

Reproduced from a note by D.J. Turner in *Surrey Archaeological Collections* LX (1963)

Water, so necessary to life, would probably have been collected in man-made or natural depressions in the land, lined with puddled clay to cut off the earth's heat and to allow dew to condense and collect. The village pond may well have started life in a similar way, as a Mesolithic dew pond. Flint tools of Mesolithic date were discovered in quite large numbers only a few hundred yards away from the pond and also at nearby Sanderstead Court to the south-east of the Parish church; during excavations in 1959 evidence was found of Mesolithic, Neolithic and Romano-British presence on this site.

The nomadic lifestyle of these earliest inhabitants of the area was dictated by the animals they hunted for food, and some of our roads may well have begun life as animal tracks which the hunters followed and compacted. Animals, particularly the larger mammals, are notorious for using consistent well-worn paths, as late 20th century residents will have discovered from the foxes that visit local gardens. It is known that the Mesolithic hunters had domesticated hunting dogs and trained them – Sanderstead's first 'dog-walkers'! To them also we almost certainly owe the knowledge of which of our native plants are edible (such as the Ramsons and Dandelion illustrated) and which are poisonous and probably also the knowledge of some of those useful for medicine and healing. They would have used plant fibres to make clothes, baskets, ropes and other useful artefacts.

Such a way of life could only be successful for relatively small groups – perhaps one or more extended families working together – sharing the work and skills required; a lifestyle based on co-operation, mutual trust and self-help, but probably without any legalistic or governmental structure.

Edible plants known to Mesolithic man. *Above:* Ramsons, *right* Dandelion.

Some 3000 years later, around 4500 BC the first farmers – the Neolithic or New Stone Age people – arrived in southern Britain. Through a chance hybrid between two common grasses which produced larger and fertile seeds, the first cereals had been discovered, and a settled existence based on growing cereals and other crops became possible. This enabled more mouths to be fed, and there was an increase in population in Neolithic times which in turn provided the manpower required for farming. Like the hunter-gatherers before them, they too have left evidence of their presence in Sanderstead, and were the first people to settle here. Their tools were still made of flint but were far more sophisticated, being designed for specific tasks: sickles, knives, primitive ploughs, quern stones for grinding corn, and also many domestic artefacts have been found in Britain. By Neolithic times the basic shape for almost all of the tools in everyday use today had been invented. In Sanderstead two polished flint axes, arrowheads, and a large number of worked flints of Neolithic date have been found.

This change from hunter-gathering to settled farming took place gradually, with the two systems overlapping for a time, but represents the most radical change in the history of humankind.

It is possible that these earliest settlers in Sanderstead mined chalk for marling their fields. The Neolithic peoples had mining technology of which the best known evidence is at Grimes Graves in Norfolk; but some of the 'dene-holes' or chalk wells found in King's Wood and elsewhere in Sanderstead may be of Neolithic date. One was excavated in 1959 by Mr. Roger Little and found to contain an 18th century horseshoe near the top, at subsequent depths medieval pottery, and finally a Mesolithic flint blade. None of these can be claimed as conclusive evidence of dating but all suggest a long history of chalk and flint extraction in Sanderstead. This ancient 'commoners' right' was incorporated into a farm lease for land adjoining King's Wood as recently as 1912.

With the discovery of metals – copper, bronze and ultimately iron, tools became even more efficient. Ploughs for example could be given metal tips which provided a more durable cutting edge, thus enabling the heavier clay soils to be worked as well as the lighter sandy or chalky soils. Metals are, however, less widely available than stone or flint, and the need to obtain them and the technology for mining the ores and smelting them, led to a more structured and acquisitive society. The evidence also points to a more aggressive stance, with homesteads defended by earthworks. Bronze Age finds in Sanderstead are few, but include a socketed bronze axe found on Riddlesdown and it has been suggested that the burial mounds found on Croham Hurst are of Bronze Age date. Across the parish border to the south at Nore Hill, near Chelsham, a defended Bronze Age homestead has recently been found.

It is, however, from the Iron Age and Romano-British period that Sanderstead can lay claim to one of the most interesting archaeological finds to the south of London.

In the woods now known as King's Wood (formerly Sanderstead Woods) on the parish boundary, a small farmstead of Romano-British date was found by Roger Little in 1955 and partially excavated. Two hut floors were found and evidence of a small burial ground which yielded four cremation urns, a child's feeding bottle and other associated pottery dating from the first and second centuries AD. Another Romano-British settlement was found in 1960 on the site of what is now Atwood Junior School. This had been built on an earlier smaller Iron Age settlement and yielded two hut floors, several rubbish pits, rotary querns, tools and pottery. There was also evidence to suggest that this settlement was connected by a prehistoric trackway to the other farmstead in King's Wood. In 1989, the opportunity to excavate the site further arose when the school was enlarged, and it was found to be even more extensive than originally thought. The evidence from the Atwood site confirms that a small community settled there from around 600 BC until the beginning of the second century AD, a period of some 700 years. The site lies alongside the present Limpsfield Road, an ancient route which was important for trade and communication. Articles discovered on the Atwood site show evidence of trade over a wide area, including imported material from the Continent. As the Limpsfield Road continues south it links together other prehistoric sites and the Roman Villa at Titsey. At Titsey Hill it crosses another old trackway, reputedly used centuries later by pilgrims travelling to Canterbury and now part of the North Downs Way. The Limpsfield Road trackway ultimately led to the important iron smelting area of the Weald.

What sort of life did these Iron Age or Celtic inhabitants of Sanderstead lead? It can only be conjecture from the artefacts that have been found on the two sites. These include:

> a lava quernstone of German origin;
> areas of burning, with silt and charcoal deposits;
> vast amounts of pottery;

Above left: Iron Age pot found at Atwood School Site - Courtesy Atwood School

Above right: Romano-British child's feeding bottle from King's Wood

Below: Children from Atwood School, each child standing in an excavated Romano-British post hole

concentrations of carbonised grain;
post holes indicating more than one large structure, and a line of post holes that may indicate a
fence, or boundary;
various objects and tools made of ferrous metal, bone, horn and flint;
a ferrous hobnail;
a whetstone;
flint arrowheads;
an almost complete Roman pottery cup
and an early Roman bronze brooch.

These finds indicate considerable domestic activity over a long period, based on the farming of cereals and other crops, animal husbandry and hunting with arrows. Even a hint of vanity or status on the part of the owner of the Roman brooch is evident.

The archaeological evidence revealed so far gives the latest date for the Iron Age settlement as the beginning of the second century AD. The subsequent history of the village from around AD 200 until AD 800 remains shrouded in mystery, but in the surviving will of Aelderman Alfred, made between AD 871 and AD 888 we have the first recorded mention of Sanderstead. A translation of part of this will reads:

'I, Aelderman Alfred command to be written and made known in this document to King Alfred and all his councillors and advisors, and likewise to my kinsmen and friends, the names of the persons to whom I most readily grant my inheritance and my bookland [1], namely my wife Waerburh and the child of us both. That is then, first 32 hides in Sanderstead and Selsdon, and 20 hides in Westerham and 30 hides in Clapham and 6 hides in Lingfield and 10 hides in Horsley and 6 hides in Nettlestead. I, Aelderman Alfred, give to Waerburh and to Ealhthryth, the child of us both, these lands after my death with livestock and with crops and with everything which belongs to those lands – and I give them 2000 swine along with the lands – if Waerburh remains unmarried as we verbally agreed. And she is to take to St. Peter's my two wergilds[2], if it be God's will that she may perform that journey. And after Waerburh's death the land at Sanderstead and Selsdon and at Lingfield is to pass uncontested to Ealhthryth. And if she has a child, that child is to succeed to the land after her; if she has no child, the nearest kin descended from her direct paternal ancestry is to succeed to the land and to the stock.'

Notes:

[1] Bookland: land not governed by inheritance custom. The owner was free to bequeath it as he chose. This type of holding was created by a title-deed called a 'book' in the vernacular.

[2] Wergild: the price that had to be paid in compensation for killing a man. The amount varied according to the dead man's rank in society.

Will of Aelderman Alfred
from Stowe Charter 20
By permission of The British Library

Note that the Ealderman's will entailed the estate, allowing the ownership to pass down through the female line. This was normal practice in Anglo-Saxon times if there were no male descendants of the same degree of kinship.

The reference to Lingfield in this will is interesting. There is strong evidence to support the theory that a strip of eastern Surrey, southwards of Croydon and bounded by two Roman roads, belonged to Kent in and before the seventh century AD. This area included Sanderstead and Selsdon. It was the practice in Kent for settlements in the north to drive their animals south to graze in the Wealden forest at certain times of the year – a practice known as 'transhumance' – and these forest grazings were known as 'denns'. It is thought that Sanderstead had a connection with Lingfield in the Weald in this way.

MAP OF EAST SURREY

based on information in Blair J, (1991). *Early Medieval Surrey*, showing the link between Sanderstead, the sub-manor of Langhurst, and Lingfield

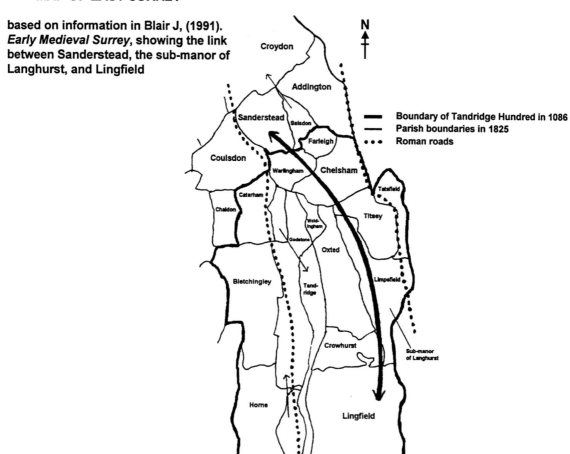

Sanderstead also had connections with Limpsfield, where the sub-manor of Langhurst was also owned in the ninth century by the Abbot of Hyde, and after the Dissolution of the Monasteries in 1539, by the Gresham family.

In this will is the earliest record also of Selsdon – or Sele's Hill – which from earliest times has been linked with Sanderstead.

EARLY SANDERSTEAD AND THE DOMESDAY RECORD

About a hundred years later, in 964 AD, we learn that Ethelfleda, the first wife of King Edgar and mother of St. Edward King & Martyr, gave the Manor of Sanderstead to the new minster at Winchester founded by King Alfred, later to become the Benedictine Abbey of St. Peter's, Hyde, and it remained in ecclesiastical hands until the Reformation in the 16th century. Very little has been found from Anglo-Saxon times: a bronze strap-end of Anglo-Saxon date was found in 1958 during excavations near Sanderstead Pond. Much earlier, the *Croydon Advertiser* of 7th March 1885 recorded the discovery of a small Anglo-Saxon cemetery containing 11 or 12 skeletons 300 yards south of Sanderstead railway station. Other burials of Saxon date were found near the junction of Riddlesdown Road and Mitchley Avenue, in the south of the parish.

There is a tradition that there was a Saxon church on the site of the present parish church of All Saints' built in the 13th century. Some axe-tooling of unknown date was found on stonework at the east end of the north aisle, and traces of older building materials, including Roman-type mortar, in the west wall. It was quite usual for older pieces of stonework to be incorporated into a newer building. There is no mention of a church in the Domesday record, but according to a chronicle of Hyde Abbey, Sanderstead had a church when Queen Ethelfleda gave the manor to the Abbey. It is however from the Domesday survey that we have a picture of the manor as it was in 1086, when it was recorded in 'William's Great Book'.

The Domesday Record

When William the Conqueror called his bishops and courtiers together during midwinter 1085 we learn from *The Anglo-Saxon Chronicle* that –

'The King had very deep speech with his counsellors about this land, how it was occupied and by what men. He then sent his men over all England into each shire, and had it made out how many hides of land were in each shire; what the King himself had in land, and in livestock on the land; what dues he had from property each twelve months from the shire; also he let it be written down how much land his archbishops had, his diocesan bishops, his abbots and his earls – what and how much each man who was holding land in England, in land, in livestock, and how much money it was worth .....'

One such Manor was Sanderstead, recorded as belonging to the Abbey of St. Peter's Winchester. Translated from the Latin, the record reads:

'In Wallington Hundred

The Abbey of St. Peter's of Winchester holds Sanderstead.

Before 1066 it answered for 18 hides, now for 5 hides.

Land for 10 ploughs. In Lordship 1;

21 villagers and 1 cottager with 8 ploughs. 4 slaves.

Woodland at 30 pigs.

Value before 1066, 100s; later £7; now £12; however, it pays £15.'

Imagine the excitement – and the suspicion – aroused in the village when they were visited by King William's team of commissioners. The local people spoke Anglo-Saxon, the commissioners would have spoken Norman-French. How easy for misunderstandings to arise, or for the villagers to withhold information they did not wish to give. Small wonder that Domesday Book is full of anomalies. That the undertaking was possible at all was due in no small measure to the administrative skill of the Anglo-Saxons, who had already divided the country into shires, hundreds and parishes. This detailed survey was completed within the astonishingly short time of one year.

Historians have puzzled for centuries over the exact interpretation of Domesday Book. How large was the Manor? A hide was originally equal to 120 acres in Saxon times, but by 1085 it had lost much of its measurement meaning and had become a tax assessment unit. A strict interpretation of the figure of 18 hides would give 2160 acres, which is not widely different from the area declared at the time of the Reformation five centuries later of 2360 acres. At the time of the Tithe Apportionment of 1844 it was given as 2245 acres.

A HISTORY OF SANDERSTEAD

How should one interpret 'woodland at 30 pigs'? It is clear from elsewhere in Domesday Book that this was the income, in pigs, to the Lord of the Manor derived from the commoners' right to pasture their pigs in the Manor woodland. In some parts of Surrey, the levy was one pig for every seven pastured, in other parts one pig in ten. If one pig in ten was the custom in Sanderstead, how much woodland was needed to support about 300 pigs? Attempts to estimate the amount of woodland in Domesday times on this basis are highly subjective, but we can be reasonably sure that Sanderstead had a fairly substantial amount of woodland at the time.

Some attempt has also been made by historians to estimate the population, on the basis of 3.5 members per family (the suggested likely average). This would give Sanderstead a population of around 80, as only the head of each family was included in the 'villagers', but it may have been larger than this. 700 years later, in the reign of George III, the population return for Sanderstead gave 204 and it remained at about that level until well into the 19th century.

The eight ploughs, or plough-teams, drawn by oxen (usually eight to a plough, equivalent in value in Saxon law to a slave) would have been shared, the community working together in co-operation to make the best use of the available resources. The open field system, with three large fields, appears to have been used in Sanderstead and each family was allocated a number of strips in these open fields. What was grown, however, was a community decision and was planned on a rotational basis. Each villager would have been expected to work for a fixed number of days each year on the Lord of the Manor's land or 'demesne', in accordance with his prerogative of 'in Lordship 1 plough'.

Under the feudal system the Lord of the Manor's rule was virtually law, and in Sanderstead it was ecclesiastical ownership, with a Bailiff or Steward of the Abbey of St. Peter's deputising for the Abbot himself. The Bailiff is mentioned in an Agreement dated 1251 between the Abbot and John de Pirlye, giving the latter rights of pasturage.

Villagers were not allowed to leave their manor without permission and although notionally 'free' tenants, in many ways they were subservient and lacking liberty. However, they had a say in the running of the Manor, being required to attend the Manor Court through which the manor was administered and business was carried out 'according to the traditional custom of the manor'. This limited to some extent the powers of the Lord and had some influence on the way the manor was run.

Village life certainly had its irksome and punitive restrictions, but on the positive side was the co-operation, self-sufficiency and mutual care by which the community shared the ups and downs of daily life in Saxon and Norman times.

SOURCES

Anglo-Saxon Chronicle

BLAIR, John (1991). *Medieval Surrey*. Surrey Archaeological Society

CUNLIFFE, B. *Iron Age Britain.* English Heritage

English Historical Documents. 2nd Edition No. 97

FARLEY, M. (1967). *Guide to Antiquities.* Bourne Society

LAING, L. & LAING, J. (1980) *The Origins of Britain.* Paladin

LITTLE, R. (1964) 'The Atwood Iron Age and Romano-British Site, Sanderstead 1960'. *Surrey Archaeological Collections* **61**

MANNING & BRAY (1809). *History of Surrey*

MORRIS, J. (Ed). *Domesday Book - Surrey.* Phillimore

Musum of London Archaeological Department (MOLAS)

Victoria County History - Surrey (1912)

Winchester Diocesan Records

Chapter 3

Life in the Manor

by Joy Gadsby and Bob Adams

The manor remained in the ownership of the Benedictine Abbey of Hyde until the Reformation, but was leased out from time to time. It is supposed to have been leased to the Saunders family in about 1250 (during the reign of Henry III), and to Walter de Stapledon, Bishop of Exeter, in 1324.

Daily life under the manorial system would have followed a regular pattern year in, year out, with most of the inhabitants of Sanderstead engaged in tilling the fields, paying their tithes to the Abbey's representative, and working the agreed number of days on the demesne land. Life was probably for the most part peaceful, but there is evidence of minor disputes between Sanderstead and neighbouring Warlingham concerning the area we know today as Hamsey Green. In 1272 the Prior of Bermondsey, who owned the Manor of Warlingham, complained that his neighbour, the Abbot of Hyde, had appropriated 16 acres of Warlingham land, plus a further rood-and-a-half elsewhere in Warlingham. In 1276 the Abbot of Hyde took the Prior of Bermondsey to court for setting up a gallows in Sanderstead – the Prior insisting that the gallows was within his own Manor of Warlingham.

The ancient Sanderstead Manor covered the same ground as the parish without Selsdon. Selsdon itself was a detached part of the Manor of Croydon, held by the Archbishop of Canterbury from the Crown. Croham Manor, first mentioned in 1287, straddled the Sanderstead/Croydon border, and the other 'manor' within Sanderstead was East Purley, with lands in the north and west of the parish. It is said to have included a house called 'The Hall', near the Rectory, almost certainly the one called the 'White House' today. By 1590 East Purley had been consolidated into the Sanderstead estates.

Whether ripples of unrest felt throughout the south-east at the time of Wat Tyler's rebellion in 1381 – and the one led a century later by Jack Cade, during which the Archbishop of Canterbury was murdered – were felt in Sanderstead we can only guess; neither is it known whether the Black Death that ravaged England in 1348/49 and which resulted in the demise of between one third and one half of the population, had a devastating effect on Sanderstead. It is clear, however, that the changes that occurred over time in the wake of this terrible plague did affect the daily lives of the villagers. The old feudal system of open-farming gradually gave way to enclosure of the common fields, a wage-based economy, and the rise of a new class of yeoman farmer of more substantial means than the common labourer; traditionally freemen and in some cases owning land freehold. Nevertheless the ownership of the Manor of Sanderstead rested firmly in the hands of Hyde Abbey, with any farmers, even wealthy families like the Ownsteads and Atwoods, being tenants rather than landowners.

It is possible to glean some insights into the state of the parish from the levying of taxes. One such tax, known as the Lay Subsidy and sometimes called the 'tenths and fifteenths tax', was raised in the later middle ages. During the 13th and 14th centuries it was an important source of revenue for the Government. The amount varied from time to time depending on the need and the willingness of Parliament to agree the tax. The tax was levied on the true value of most of the moveable goods of a household, including farm animals and implements, and food stores. However a single standardised value was usually applied to each sort of domestic animal in an area, regardless of its age or condition. A few items were exempt; these included the armour of knights and their riding horses because of their use in war, and the jewels and fine clothes of the gentry and their ladies, to preserve the distinction and dignity of the knightly classes. Also exempt were the poor. Those with moveable property worth less than 10 shillings were not assessed for the tax.

All Saints', Sanderstead, showing the wall paintings on each side of the east window

Above: Piscina in All Saints', one of the church's oldest features.

Left: Drawing of the 14th century wall paintings, depicting (far left) St. Edmund, King and Martyr and Edmund, Archbishop of Canterbury in the 13th century.

LIFE IN THE MANOR

Sanderstead seems to have been a relatively wealthy parish. In 1332, 13 inhabitants were assessed for a total of 52s.9d compared to the 12 inhabitants of neighbouring Selsdon who were assessed for 16s.2d. Four years later Sanderstead was assessed for 3 shillings more and Selsdon for 9 pence more. For comparison, Croydon was assessed for £9.0s.9½d and Coulsdon for 17s.9¾d.

The taxpayers of Sanderstead included Johanne de Westpurle and Reginaldo de Purle. These are very early indications of the local place name Purley, which formed part of the parish of Sanderstead at that time. The Selsdon names included Is' de Ouenestede, an ancestor of John Ownstead who was Lord of the Manor during the reign of Elizabeth I. The other Sanderstead names were Willelmo Kyng (after whom King's Wood, Sanderstead, may have taken its name – an accidental misplacement by the Ordnance Survey in the 19th century), Willelmo and Ricardo ate Hoke, Roberto de Chapman, Johanne Totenham, Johanne le Hayward, Willelmo Messager, Johanne Ricard, Johanne de Cattele and Thomas le Cartere.

The one certain evidence of vitality in medieval Sanderstead is the Parish Church of All Saints'. The present building was begun in about 1230, during the reign of Henry III, with the tower being added about 1310. The walls are of local knapped flint, with more solid stone at the corners, and the church was originally roofed with wooden shingles. The style is Early English, and originally it had a nave, a raised chancel and a small aisle on both north and south sides. In a pillar supporting the north-east corner of the nave is a small piscina, thought to date from 1230, suggesting that there may have been a small chapel on that side. Later evidence suggests it was dedicated to St. Catherine.

The building is unsophisticated; no two arches are exactly alike in height or width, and it was customary to decorate churches outside and inside with coloured lime-wash. Some evidence has been found that this was the case here.

In 1936 two wall paintings were discovered on the east wall, on either side of the high altar, and these have been dated to the 14th century. They depict St. Edmund, King of East Anglia who was martyred by the Danes in 870 – a saint much revered in medieval England – and Edmund, Archbishop of Canterbury in the 13th century at the time the church was built. It has been suggested that the paintings were possibly intended as a link between an earlier Saxon church dedicated to St. Edmund and the 13th century church built during Archbishop Edmund's time.

There may have been other wall paintings. The services would have been conducted in Latin and as the congregation would have been largely illiterate pictures would probably have been used to convey the Christian message. The church will also have been at the centre of village life, used as a meeting place as well as a place of worship. The name of the church was originally 'Alhalon' but this gradually changed to All Saints' from about 1489.

The wooden door at the main entrance to the church today is almost certainly the 13th century original. It is built from a double layer of heavy oak planks,

Stone figure in nave of All Saints' Church, thought to represent one of the 13th century masons.

Drawing by Wendy Davison

placed vertically on one side and horizontally on the other, fixed by iron bolts, not nails, and with a large medieval lock and key. Parishioners have entered the church past it for over 750 years to worship.

Did local craftsmen build the church? Alas, it is not known who the masons were, but the likenesses of their faces in stone peer down at us from the tops of the pillars in the nave. Almost certainly local materials were used, and local builders and craftsmen involved to a greater or lesser degree. They built simply but they built to last, and we still enjoy the benefits of their craftsmanship today.

SOURCES

BRIGGS, Asa (1994). *A Social History of England.* Weidenfeld & Nicolson.

HARGREAVES, M. (1977) *Sanderstead and its Parish Church.* Bourne Society *Local History Records*, **XVI**

MANNING & BRAY (1809). *History of Surrey.*

SAALER, M. (1989) *East Surrey Manors.* Bourne Society

Figure of queen in south porch of All Saints' Church, possibly 14th century queen of Henry III

Drawing by Gwyneth Fookes after a drawing dated 1910

Chapter 4

Tudor Times

by Joy Gadsby and Francis Davison

The earliest memorials in All Saints' Church are two brasses, one to John and Dyones Atwood who died in 1525 and 1530 respectively, and the other to Nicholas Atwood who died in 1586. Some light on 16th century life and times is shed by the will of Dyones, a transcript of part of which reads as follows:

> 'In the name of God Amen. The XXth day of August the yere of our Lord God MCCCCCXXX, I Denys Atwood, layte wyf of John Atwood of Saunderstede in the counte of Surr and dioc. of Winchester widow beyng in good mynde and pfyte remembrance laud be to God make thys testament and last wyll in manner and form following – ffyrst I bequeth my soull to allmyghty God to the virgin Mary and to all the company of hevyn and my body to be buryed wtin the church of Saunderstede before the aulter of Saynt Kateryne. Itm I bequeth unto the hye alter of the same churche of Saundersted IIIId. Item to the mother churche of Winchester IIIId. Item. I bequeth unto the buylldyng of the yelle *(aisle)* of Seynt Kateryn wtin the said churche of Saunderstede VII£. Item. I bequeth unto Richard Atwood my son VII£. I bequeth unto John Atwoode my yongest son XLs. Item I bequeth unto Agnes my daughter my best gowne and best kyrtell. I bequeth unto John Atwood my secunde son otherwyse callyd Hewson XL shepe wt the ffetherbed complet wt all that longyth thereto also the same John Atwood to have halfe brasse and pewter and my sonne Richard Atwood to have the other halfe. Itm I bequeth to the syling (ceiling) of the body of the said church of Saunderstede X anyell nobylls *(a nobyll was worth 6s.8d)*. Itm I bequeth to a branch of brasse to bere a lyght for Seynt Kateryn XVs. Itm. I bequeth 2s to have V trentall as the Pson wyll dispose yt. (A trentall – 30 masses rehearsed for 30 days). Itm. I bequeth John Atwood the elder VII£. Itm I bequeth also to the said John Atwood XLs in the hands of Henry Atwood. I constitute and ordeyn my executor of thys my last wyll John Atwoode the elder and the Pson to be oversear of thys my last wyll. ....'

Probate inventories of the period rarely mention money. The economy was based largely on self sufficiency and bartering, with money spent only for household goods and clothes not made locally. The amount of money bequeathed by Dyones was relatively large for the time, but of value also were the 40 sheep left to her son John and the gown left to her daughter Agnes. Was it the same gown as that depicted on her memorial brass? If so it was fashionable and sumptuous, with narrow sleeves with fur cuffs elegantly split, and a beautiful, low belt with a triple rose fastening and bells dangling from it – the latter a fashion accessory that was very popular on the Continent at that time. She also wore a gable head-dress and her shoes had rounded toes and platform soles.

Dyones' will predates the Reformation, as can be sensed by the references made to the saints and to religious rites but it is interesting that the two Rectors who held office between 1551 and 1590 each served under both Catholic and Protestant monarchs.

In 1535 Henry VIII ordered a valuation to be made of all church property, and a translation of the entry for Sanderstead from his *Valor Ecclesiasticus* is as follows –

> 'A valuation of church property taken during the reign of Henry VIII, with the authority of the King.
>
> Rectory of Sanderstead, in the diocese of Winchester. Edward Prestlond sworn there.

**Monumental brasses in
All Saints' Church**

Left: John and Dyones Atwood,
1525

Above: Seven sons and three
daughters of Nicholas
Atwood

He presented a schedule in the presence of the aforesaid commissioners at Godstone, in the county of Surrey, on August 11th in the 27th year of the reign of our present king, Henry VIII (1535) of the said rectory as he assessed it, as follows:

The dwelling-house of the rectory there, with a garden and four acres, is worth annually: 5s.6d

Value of profits of dairy produce and small tithes: 4s.0d

Tithe of eggs: 10d; of rabbits: 6s. 8d. Annual total: 7s.6d

Value of wax and honey annually: 4d

Tithe of hemp and flax: 2½d

Tithes of wool and lambs annually: 46s.8d

Tithes of grain annually, namely: three quarters of wheat: 20s at 6s.8d a quarter: 14 quarters of barley: 26s.8d at 3s.4d (a quarter): 66s.8d

Tithe of beans and vetch: 10s.

Offerings at the four main festivals of the year annually: 5s.

The churchyard there, annual value: 6d

Tithe of apples: 4d; of piglets: 12d; with offerings by donation: 2s. Total: 3s.4d

      Total: £7. 9s.8½d

Deductions:

Payment to the archdeacon of Surrey: 7s.7½d

To the lord bishop of Winchester for church dues: 2s.1d

   Total: 9s.8½d

   Net value: £7. 0s.0d

   Tenth part: 14s.0d'

From this valuation it appears that half of the value of the Estate at that time came from the cultivation of cereal crops and one third from sheep and wool. It is also interesting to note the relative value of rabbits, which were an important source of food in the care of a Warrener, compared to that of pigs. Looking forward, by the 19th century the price of grain at the time of the Tithe Apportionment (see chapter 7) had increased eight-fold, but the relative values of wheat and barley remained the same.

The Dissolution of the Monasteries followed, in 1539. Shortly before this, Hyde Abbey's possessions in Surrey were let to Sir John Gresham for the yearly rent of one red rose. As soon as the monks had signed the Deed giving up their lands to the King, the Crown granted them to Sir John in return for £79 and a small annual rent. He thus became the owner of the Manor of Sanderstead as well as of other properties in the County. In 1547 Sir John was elected Lord Mayor of London, the first of several Sanderstead citizens to hold this office.

Sir John died in 1556 but the Manor remained in the Gresham family until 1591 when it was sold by his grandson, Richard, to John Ownstead the younger. However, this transfer was not finalised until 1594 on payment of a fine of nearly £9 for not having obtained the necessary licence in advance. At the time of the transfer the manorial lands were specified as:

  800 acres of land (i.e. arable)

   50 acres of meadow,

  500 acres pasture,

  300 acres woodland and

  700 acres furze and heath;

    in total 2350 acres.

Another important source of village history dating back to Tudor times is provided by the Parish Records. These were instituted in the reign of Henry VIII by his Chancellor, Thomas Cromwell, and from them we know the names of some of the villagers. The earliest baptisms recorded are for Richard Curteise in 1565 and Joanna Thorne in 1566. The first wedding was that between Henricus Woodstocke and Alicia Thornton, the entries being made in Latin. The Ownstead family also figures largely in these earliest records.

John Ownstead has a very fine monument in All Saints' Church from which we learn that he was 'servant to ye most excellent Princess and our dread sovereign Queene Elizabeth and Serjeant of Her Majestie's carriage by ye space of 40 years'. He must have been an astute and wise servant to have remained in Elizabeth's favour for so long.

In the time of Elizabeth I Sanderstead still had an open field system, with three common fields – north, east and west fields – the latter

Memorial to John Ownstead

† 1600

commemorated in a modern road name. Common land for grazing remained at Hamsey Heath, which straddled the parish boundary between Sanderstead and Warlingham. Overgrazing was prevented, in theory at least, by 'stinting' – a fixed number of animals per tenement and fixed time when grazing was allocated. From this we derive the expressions' to do one's stint' and 'don't stint yourself' although the circumstances of usage have changed.

Not surprisingly there was a certain amount of cheating! In 1575 the matter was taken to court and as a result the tenants of Sanderstead were allocated 20 acres of common land called Hamsey Heath and the tenants of Warlingham were granted land on Riddlesdown. Independent surveyors were to measure out the 20 acres of Hamsey Heath with 'metes, boundes and hedges'. There is no direct evidence of when the open fields were enclosed, but indications from old maps and the apparent age and species richness of some of the hedges *(see chapter 17)* suggest that these fields were enclosed well before 1700. Enclosure was common in late Tudor times especially in sheep-farming regions such as the North Downs. It also seems that, unlike the later Parliamentary enclosures, the entire manor became the property of the Lord of the Manor when it was enclosed and that those who had previously supplemented their livelihood from grazing their animals on the common land lost their right to do so. This would have meant considerable hardship for the individuals concerned.

Whilst the majority of households in the village were engaged in agriculture and sheep farming, the increasingly important merchanting trade had its representatives among the few wealthy Sanderstead families most of whom were members of the Merchant Taylors Company and were linked together by marriage as well as by business connection. Foremost among these were the Atwoods, the St. Johns and the Mellishes.

The oldest secular building in Sanderstead is 'The White House', the earliest remaining part of which is timber-framed and reputed to be of early 16th century date. There are, however, features inside the house that

'The White House', on record at least from the 14th century

suggest it may have been built on a much earlier foundation. It was probably originally the home of a wealthy farmer and is possibly the house formerly called 'The Hall', or 'Copt Hall'. In 1620 the name was referred to as one of the residences in Sanderstead and Purley of Richard Mellish, the Sanderstead property being described as 'near the parsonage'. It does not appear to have been called White House Farm or 'The White House' before the 19th century. The Mellishes inhabited Sanderstead for several generations and were wealthy merchants. It was, however, the Atwood family who were to dominate Sanderstead life for the next 300 years.

**An interior of 'The White House', August 1937,
from an article in *Ideal Home* magazine**

A 'Guess-map' of Elizabethan Sanderstead appears overleaf

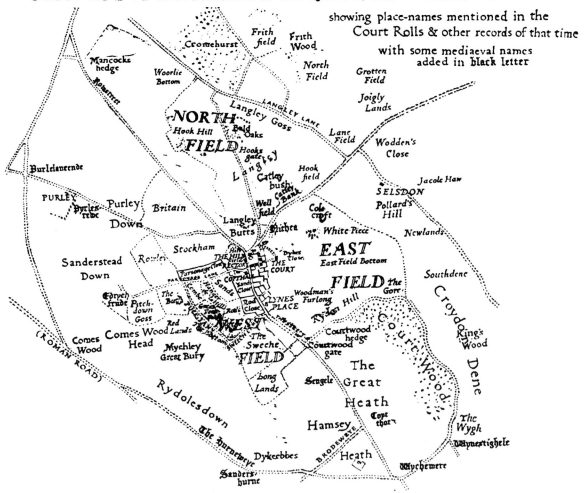

GUESS-MAP OF SANDERSTEAD IN QUEEN ELIZABETH'S REIGN

showing place-names mentioned in the
Court Rolls & other records of that time

with some mediaeval names
added in black letter

SOURCES

All Saints' Church Parish Records

CALEY, J. & HUNTER, J. (Eds.) *Valor Ecclesiasticus*

Public Record Office

SAALER, M. (1989). *East Surrey Manors*. Bourne Society

Surrey County Record Office, Kingston-upon-Thames.

Chapter 5

Civil War, Regicide, and the Aftermath

by Joy Gadsby and Bob Adams

John Ownstead died in 1600 at the age of 66 and left his estates first to his wife, and then one third to his two sisters and two thirds to his cousin Harman Atwood. By 1618 Harman had acquired the whole estate and thus began the long association between the Atwood family and the Manor of Sanderstead.

Harman Atwood was a lawyer of Cliffords Inn, London. He had at least five sons and one daughter, Olive, who later built the Rectory that once stood where the Rectory Court flats are now. Harman's first son John was by his first wife, Elizabeth Lawrence and it is from this marriage that the Wigsell side of the family later inherited the manor. Elizabeth died in 1604 and Harman married Joan King, who was related to the Leigh family of neighbouring Addington. He had four more sons by Joan, the first of whom, named King Atwood after his mother's maiden name, entered the Church and was for over 40 years Rector of Sanderstead.

The Armorial Achievement of Harman Atwood

Harman Atwood appears to have been a caring man, and left a legacy of 20s. per annum (a considerable sum in those days), part to go to provide for the poor of the parish and part to the Rector on condition that a sermon be preached in perpetuity on the Sunday nearest 5th November 'in thankful remembrance of God's mercy in delivering church and state from the horrid treason of Gunpowder Plot'; this condition is still fulfilled – nominally at least – by the Rectors of All Saints'. Harman Atwood died in 1653 and was succeeded as Lord of the Manor by his fourth son, also called Harman. To this Harman we owe the almshouses at Warlingham, which still serve their original purpose of providing a home for two elderly residents of Warlingham (whose Manor Harman also held) and one each for Chelsham and Sanderstead. Strict rules applied to the choice of residents, who had to be deserving, honest, god-fearing, and of sober habits.

There was a 17th century tax that throws some light on Sanderstead at this period. After the Restoration of the Monarchy in 1660 one of the major sources of revenue to King Charles' government was the Hearth Tax. The tax was levied between 1662 and 1689, and was paid by the occupiers of houses at the rate of 2 shillings a year for each hearth in a house. Half was payable on Lady Day (25th March) and the other half on Michaelmas Day (29th September). The poor were exempt. In 1664 there were 15 houses with 62 hearths in Sanderstead. Of these, three houses with one hearth each were occupied by poor people and were exempt. Another house with two hearths was exempt because it was empty. The remaining 11 houses with 57 hearths between them paid a total of £5.14s.0d that year. Harman Atwood paid £2 of this in respect of his 16 hearths at 'Sanderstead Court' and four at another house in Purley.

It is possible to attempt to estimate the population of a village from the number of its households. In this period the average size of a household is generally taken to be 4.75 persons, and this would suggest that the population of Sanderstead would be about 70. It may, however, have been more than this since exemptions are not included and the parish registers contain many more than 70 names.

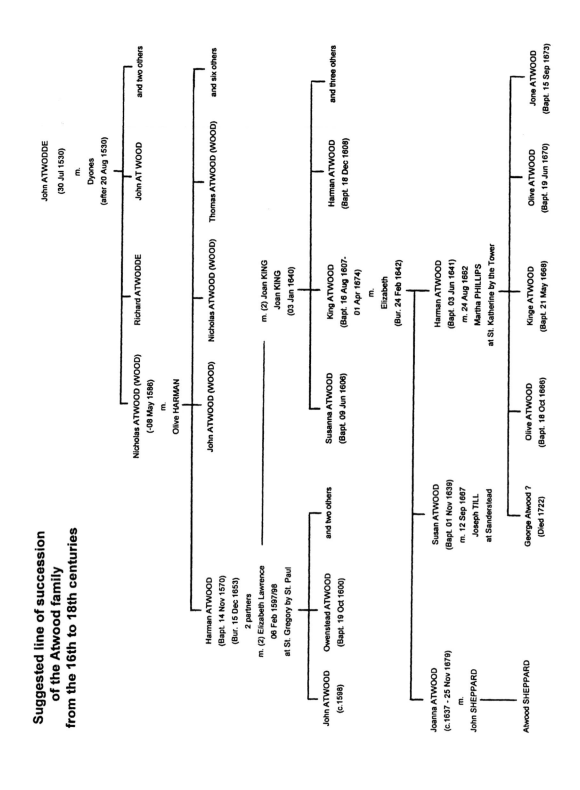

Suggested line of succession
of the Atwood family
from the 16th to 18th centuries

REGICIDE, CIVIL WAR AND ITS AFTERMATH

In 1676 Harman completed the rebuilding of 'Sanderstead Court', which included a Great Hall occupying two storeys, and supported on fluted columns with Corinthian capitals. A secret chamber is said to have been discovered in the 1890s behind the chimney in the Great Hall, and this has given rise to stories of a secret passage between 'Sanderstead Court' and 'The White House' and, by implication, to involvement in smuggling. Certainly smuggling was rife in the 17th and 18th centuries, but it hardly equates with what we know of Harman's character and abstemious disposition. The passage, if indeed it existed, may well have been a precautionary escape route should troubled times, so recently experienced, return. Alas, Harman cannot have had much time to enjoy the house as he died in the year that the new building was completed. The house, however, remained in all its glory until accidentally destroyed by fire in 1957.

Sanderstead Court, rebuilt by Harman Atwood in 1676, photographed in the 1920s

Of the other notable families in Sanderstead, the Mellish family appears in the parish records from 1573-1707. Henry Mellish, who died in 1677 was, according to his memorial in All Saints' Church, a merchant of the Levant Company.

How far the events leading up to the Civil War of 1642, the war itself, the austere years of the Commonwealth and the more relaxed attitudes that accompanied the Restoration of the Monarchy affected the ordinary villagers of Sanderstead can only be guessed. The merchanting families, with their connections with the City of London, almost certainly will have supported the Parliamentary cause. During the Commonwealth one important resident, living at Purley Bury, was Major Lewis Audley, a young officer in Cromwell's Model Army who served under Sir Thomas Fairfax. Audley seems to have risen rapidly to a position of considerable influence. On leaving the army he was appointed Justice of the Peace and several marriages were solemnised at his house, only being entered in the parish records after the Restoration. His first wife Mary, widow of Ralph Hawtrey of Middlesex, has a very fine altar tomb in Carrera marble in All Saints' Church and was obviously greatly loved. Her maiden name was Bedell, and her father too was a Merchant Taylor with business connections with the Atwoods and Mellishes. Unusually for the times the same Rector, the Revd. King Atwood, was the incumbent throughout the whole of this turbulent period, having served from 1630 during the reign of Charles I to 1674, 14 years after the Restoration of Charles II.

Sketchline of the descent of the Sanderstead Estate from Atwood through Wigsell to Arkwright. 18th - 20th century.

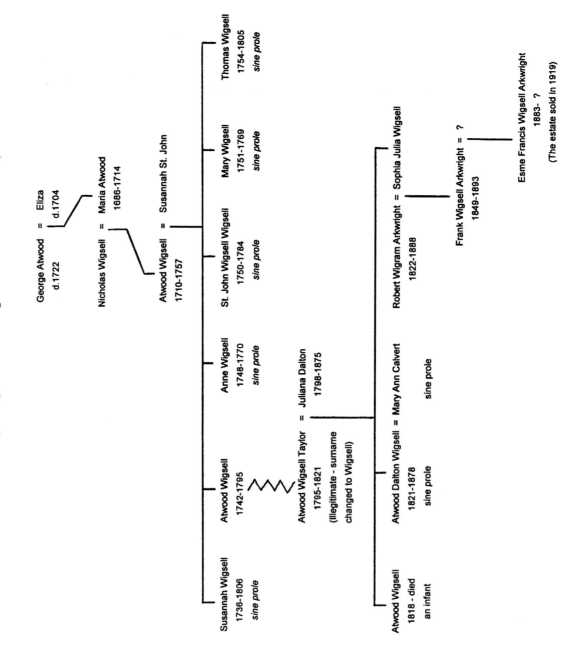

George Atwood
d.1722
=
Eliza
d.1704

Nicholas Wigsell
=
Maria Atwood
1686-1714

Atwood Wigsell
1710-1757
=
Susannah St. John

Susannah Wigsell
1736-1806
sine prole

Atwood Wigsell
1742-1795

Anne Wigsell
1748-1770
sine prole

St. John Wigsell Wigsell
1750-1784
sine prole

Mary Wigsell
1751-1769
sine prole

Thomas Wigsell
1754-1805
sine prole

Atwood Wigsell Taylor
1795-1821
(Illegitimate - surname changed to Wigsell)
=
Juliana Dalton
1798-1875

Atwood Wigsell
1818 - died
an infant

Atwood Dalton Wigsell
1821-1878
sine prole
=
Mary Ann Calvert
sine prole

Robert Wigram Arkwright
1822-1888
=
Sophia Julia Wigsell

Frank Wigsell Arkwright
1849-1893
=
?

Esme Francis Wigsell Arkwright
1863- ?
(The estate sold in 1919)

Memorial to George Mellish, † 1693
(detail below)

The shrouded effigy of Maria Audley,
wife of Major Lewis Audley, † 1655

**17th century memorials in
All Saints' Church, Sanderstead**

A HISTORY OF SANDERSTEAD

There is evidence that the old Anglican liturgy, banned elsewhere under Cromwell, continued without a break at All Saints'. Was this Mary Audley's influence? (Her son by her first marriage, John Hawtrey, was Rector here from 1674-1678). Or was it due to the fact that Lewis Audley was sympathetic, having himself been ordained Deacon in the Anglican church before joining Cromwell's army?

There is no evidence that the Plague of 1665 greatly affected Sanderstead, although there were many deaths from it in Croydon, only three miles away. The Great Fire of London that followed in 1666 would have been seen from the top of Sanderstead Hill, and as a result of that fire there was a gradual change away from timber-built towards brick-built houses. Building in brick was made compulsory in towns and cities and gradually filtered down to the more rural areas, so that every village eventually had its own brickworks.

A local bricklayer, Mr. Burrowes – who died in 1683 – left the following possessions according to a surviving probate inventory:

> 'A true and perfect Inventory of all and singular ye goods chattels and debts of John Burrowes of Sanderstead in ye County of Surrey bricklayer

Imprimis	In the Hall a little brasse and a little pewter, some wooden ware and other small things	£1 10s. 0d
Item	In the Chamber over ye hall bed and bedding 5 chests and some lumber	£2 5s. 0d
Item	In ye next roome: bedstead, bed and boulster	10s. 0d
Item	Wearing apparel	5s. 0d
Item	Lumber	1s. 0d
Item	due from Sarah Ffearne and John Ffearne by Bond dated August 18 1677 principall money	£20 0s. 0d
Item	due from Mr. Andrew Smith principall money due by Bill obligatory dated April 3 1680 or thereabouts	£5 0s. 0d
Item	from Elizabeth Clasow principall money by Bond dated Jany. 1 1679	£10 0s. 0d
	Summne totalis	£39 11s. 0d'

By the 18th century local brickmaking was well established, the brickyard being shown on John Rocque's Map of Surrey of 1764 at the edge of Sanderstead Woods, now called King's Wood. Examples of locally made bricks can still be seen in the 'Old Forge' in Limpsfield Road (now the Parish Room of the Church of the Holy Family) and in the small row of cottages opposite Sanderstead Parade, which are believed to be of about the same date – towards the end of the 18th century. The cottages are built of local flint but have a brick 'lacing course' inserted to prevent the walls from bulging, the doors and windows are strengthened with brick surrounds and the chimneys too are of brick.

The wool trade was declining from its earlier importance at the time of Elizabeth I, so much so that a law was passed in 1678 that 'no corpse except dying of plague, shall be buried in anything other than sheep's wool'. The parish records have several references to this. George Mellish, for example, who died in 1693 was 'buried in velvet', whilst in 1761 Mary Atwood was buried 'in linnen' – a transgression of the law that would have incurred a penalty of about £5. The law was not repealed until 1814.

Nor did the slave trade pass Sanderstead by. In 1772 the baptism of 'Mr. St. John's black' is recorded. How well he treated his slave we cannot tell, but at least Mr. St. John had a care for his spiritual welfare.

Notable old buildings in Sanderstead

The Forge, dating from the 18th century, now used by the Catholic Church of the Holy Family.

Sanderstead Rectory, believed to have been built by Olive Atwood, from a painting by J. Hassell (early 19th century, when the Rectory was occupied by Revd. John Courtney).   Now demolished.

'Purley Bury House', dating from the 17th century

A HISTORY OF SANDERSTEAD

In the Parliamentary election of 1710, the Surrey Poll Books of Knights of the Shire – the only people eligible to vote – show the following voters as resident in Sanderstead:

Henry Bowyer

George Atwood

William Buckle

John Atwood (This John Atwood inherited the Sanderstead Estate from his father George in 1722.)

In 1727 the Sanderstead voters were:

Phillip Wood (recorded as having land in Banstead)

Daniell Phillips (recorded as having land in Banstead)

George Quiddington (who also had land in Warlingham)

John Wood (who had land in Nutfield)

John Woodstock (land in Farley) and

John Atwood.

These Sanderstead names are very close to each other in the certified fair copy of the 1727 Poll Book in Croydon Library. The election was at Guildford and it is quite possible that they travelled together to vote, as electors from other locations are scattered randomly throughout the list. Were they of one mind? What did they talk about on the way? In any event, the two successful parliamentary candidates were Arthur Onslow and Thomas Scawen.

In 1744 John Griffithies is the only voter shown as of Sanderstead, and the 1780 Poll Book shows Atwood Wigsell and Thomas Wigsell.

By the end of the 18th century another important family, the Smiths, had moved south from Nottingham and settled in the area, eventually purchasing Selsdon Park in 1809. In 1658 Thomas Smith founded in Nottingham one of the earliest banks, predating the Bank of England by 36 years. His descendants extended the banking business to London. Through the Smiths there is a royal connection of which Sanderstead and Selsdon are justly proud. Frances Dora Smith, daughter of Oswald, married the 13th Earl of Strathmore and consequently became the great-grandmother of Queen Elizabeth II.

The Smith family was prolific, and its memorials are to be found in the church and churchyard of All Saints', together with those of some of their faithful servants. The church clock was given by a member of the Smith family in 1844 and bears the words *Pereunt et Imputantur* which may be translated as 'The hours perish and are laid to our account'.

A description of life in the village at the end of the 18th century has been left by T. Harding, who published his *Twelve Hours Perambulation of the Rural Beauties of Sanderstead* in 1798. A quotation from this describes Sanderstead as:

'Situated on a spacious eminence in the southern district of Surrey, at a small distance from Croydon, is the village of Sanderstead; remarkable not only for the salubrity of its air and the beauty of its scenery (which is of the most romantic and perspective kind) and likewise for its seeming seclusion from the busy bustle of country towns; its almost inaccessible sides towards Croydon are partly concealed by the luxuriance of woods and shrubberies, copses etc. and in the midst of this cluster arises the spire of the village Church in aweful and unadorn'd sublimity, and this beautiful and rural village with its cottages, villas and herds, presents to the view of the spectator the most pleasing scene of rural tranquility.

'Its peaceful inhabitants, ignorant of the many wants which luxury excites, find, comprised in the spot of their nativity every joy they can imagine, and convenience they can desire. Healthy, frugal and laborious, they wake with the earliest dawn, and repair with cheerfulness to their several occupations in the field.

'Animated by the desire of supporting their families, they pursue their tasks with ardour throughout the day; and when the sun descends below the horizon, retire to their respective habitations with delight, satisfied with the necessaries of life, they enjoy with thankfulness the homely meal which awaits them, and happy in the endearing caresses of the Wives of their choice, and the children of their wishes, sink into that repose which industry invokes and contentment affords.'

This idyllic picture is probably not entirely how the villagers themselves would have described life in 18th century Sanderstead!

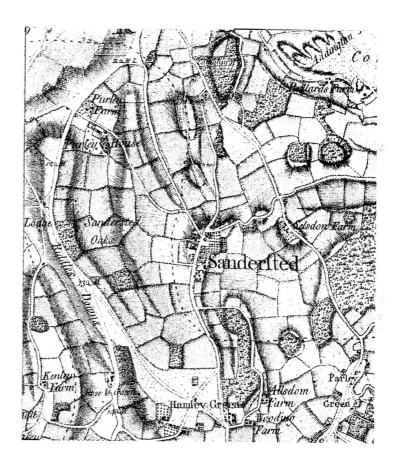

A Detail from Rocque's map of Surrey (1764) showing Sanderstead.

SOURCES

All Saints' Church Parish Records

Croydon Local Studies Library

DENDY, W. (1905-7). *History & Antiquities of the Parish of Sanderstead*

HARDING, T. (1798). *Twelve Hours Perambulations of the Rural Beauties of Sanderstead*

Nottingham Record Office (Smith and Mellish families)

Surrey County Probate Records

THARBY, W.G. (1966). 'Sanderstead'. Bourne Society *Local History Records* **5**

TUTT, D. (1975) 'The Warlingham Almshouses'. Bourne Society *Local History Records* **14**

SANDERSTEAD IN 1843

taken from the plan annexed to the tithe award

Chapter 6

The 19th Century – An Estate Village

by Bob Adams

The Wigsells

The dominant family, for good and ill, in the life of the village during the 19th century continued to be the Atwoods through the Wigsell line. Their dominance, which extended to every part of village life, only ended at the beginning of the 20th century with the break-up of the estate and encroaching development along the main routes out of Croydon. Apart from the times when the squire was also the rector, the family appears to have rarely lived in the village and 'Sanderstead Court' was let to tenants. Nevertheless they were not absentee or negligent landlords but took an active, paternalistic and dominating interest in local life. Long after the family had left – as will be seen later – its influence still pervaded the village.

Succession was not straightforward during this century, and the estate rarely passed from father to son. Nevertheless it was entailed and was handed on within the extended family. The Wigsells had acquired the estate from the Atwoods by inheritance through the female line. They still used the old family name of Atwood in each subsequent generation so as to emphasise the continuity of their title to the estate. They also adopted the Atwood's 'Axe-in-Hand' crest as part of their armorial bearings.

The first Wigsell Squire was Thomas Wigsell who inherited the estate from his uncle John, the last Atwood. Thomas had no children and when he died in 1778, the estate passed in turn to the children of his deceased brother, the Revd. Thomas Wigsell who until his death in 1757, had been Rector of Sanderstead. These children, Atwood, then the second Revd. Thomas, who also was Rector of Sanderstead, and finally Susannah, all died without legitimate children. After Susannah, the estate passed to Atwood Wigsell Taylor, then still a minor and the illegitimate son of Atwood Wigsell and Mary Taylor. The young man inherited the estate on the condition that he adopted the Wigsell surname and arms. He became Atwood Wigsell Wigsell.

He also was briefly Rector of the parish but died in 1827 when the estate descended to his infant son, Atwood Dalton Wigsell who was born in Florence a few weeks after the death of his father. This Atwood Wigsell was the squire all his life but despite marrying, he had no children. Therefore when he died in 1878 the estate passed to his sister's son, Frank Wigsell Arkwright, and later to her grandson Esme Arkwright in whose time the estate was broken up in the early 20th century.

The Village

The Wigsell family owned the village and the farmers were the family's tenants. The family appointed the Rector and indeed – as we have seen – at the start of the century the Rector was either the Squire himself or a close relative. Later, when the Randolphs became Rectors, the links between the Manor and the Rectory became those of long-standing friendship or a distant family connection rather than the close blood relationship of previous incumbents. In Sanderstead, therefore, the structure of Victorian rural life, the landowner, the farmers and the church were all firmly under the control of the Squire's family.

Throughout the 19th century, the Wigsells were major landowners in the county, and were one of the 12 largest landowners in non-metropolitan Surrey. The family's seat, 'Sanderstead Court', and almost half of its estates were in Sanderstead, where it owned 1839 acres or 85% of the parish. A contemporary estimate in 1870 puts the gross rentals from the Sanderstead estate alone at over £6000. The estates also extended into a number of adjacent parishes and beyond. At the start of the century, the remainder of the parish, mainly the northern part was owned by a small number of other private individuals but was subsequently taken over by two local charities, the Trustees of the Croydon Hospital and the Trustees of Eli Davy's Almshouse. Later, the London and Brighton Railway Company owned land for its tracks and some adjacent areas. The only other landowners were the Rector, who held the 18 acres of glebe land, and Mr John Budgen, who owned just over a quarter of an acre near the parish boundary with Warlingham, on which stood two cottages. Mr Budgen did not live in the parish.

It is evident from the late-18th Century Land Tax Returns, the Tithe Apportionment of 1843 and the later records of land ownership that during this period Sanderstead was an estate village. The land was extensively farmed but was let to just a few tenant farmers. Without any other independent people with a long-term interest in the parish, the village consisted mainly of hired hands who appear to have stayed awhile before moving on to other places.

Farms in the parish were much larger than was usual in the rest of the country at that time. One of the largest was Borough Farm, on the site of the present 'Do it All' store, where two Robert Russells, father and son, farmed some 600 acres for many years until the middle of the century. The other farms, though smaller, were also much larger than was usual for the time and were managed from farmsteads either in Sanderstead, such as White House Farm, or in an adjacent parish, such as Fox Farm. Land to the north of the parish that was not owned by the Wigsells, was similarly let to only a very few tenants.

The structure of the village reflected the way the parish was farmed. There was no inn or village green – only the Parish Church and the Manor House, 'Sanderstead Court', at the junction of the road to Selsdon and Addington with the road from Croydon that ran through the village, gave any semblance of a village centre. Even the parish church was at one stage enclosed by the walls surrounding 'Sanderstead Court' – with the Rectory on the outside. The cottages in the village were scattered around 'Sanderstead Court' and the large farms, and were used for the labourers and servants employed there. Tied housing such as this ensured that occupancy of the cottages, and hence residence in the village, was conditional upon continued employment in the parish.

How long Sanderstead had been a village with no inn is unclear. There is a reference to 'John Woodstock of the Berehows' in 1552, but the Atwood and Wigsell families were abstemious and refused to allow any property on their estate to serve as a public house. In this respect, the families' influence still pervades the life of Sanderstead. This is because covenants imposed on the land ban a public house. It is possible that these covenants could only be removed by an Act of Parliament. So the traditional village remains 'dry' even though, technically, as a result of changes made in 1995 to the boundary of the London Borough of Croydon, *The Good Companions*, formerly in Warlingham is now within Sanderstead.

Purley Downs, near Croydon 1885

- a painting by T. Whittle

(from Purley Downs Road looking north-west across Brighton Road.)

Courtesy of Croydon Library

Purley Oaks, pre-1925. A painting by Ethel Hall. Courtesy of Croydon Library

The trifoliate window in All Saints' Church

showing the arms of –

The diocese of Winchester

Wigsell   Courtney

The Church

The Squire appointed the Rector of the parish church and the incumbents at the beginning of the century were usually members of his family, sometimes even the Squire himself. However, from 1835 to 1881, the position was held first by John Courtney, then John Honywood Randolph and then his son John Randolph. John Honywood Randolph was the son of an eminent scholar and clergyman who had been Bishop of London. The Randolphs were not close relatives of the Wigsells but there may have been a family connection as there is a common device on their coats of arms. Atwood Dalton Wigsell and the younger John Randolph were contemporaries and were friends from boyhood.

The living was a well paid one and following the commutation of the Tithes gave the incumbent almost £400 a year plus the income from the 18 acres of glebe land which lay where Glebe Hyrst is now. The Randolphs, who had incomes from other sources, including an estate in Essex, lived in some style and maintained a household consisting of a number of servants.

The parish church of All Saints' was refurbished in 1846 when the galleries were removed. £85 was spent on the work at the church at this time financed by a church rate which raised over £100. After the refurbishment, the church had seating for 200 people, which was adequate for the population of the time. All the places were free. In 1851, the Rector John Randolph senior considered it an impertinence of the government to enquire about the size of his congregation in the Ecclesiastical Census and refused to give the information requested.

In 1877, in support of a campaign for reform of the finances of the Church of England, the anonymous 'Argus' column in the *Croydon Advertiser* chose the younger John Randolph as an example of what he saw as contemporary clerical greed. This was a major theme in mid-Victorian England and was at the heart of Anthony Trollope's novel, *Barchester Towers*. John Randolph was criticised because he received a much higher salary for the not very onerous work as Rector of Sanderstead than the curates in charge of some nearby churches who had much heavier workloads. Argus claimed that one of the reasons that John Randolph had very little to do was because there was no public house in the parish!

John Randolph responded:

'Sir, I consider that you have exceeded in a most unwarrantable manner what is called the liberty of the Press in allowing your anonymous correspondent, 'Argus', to drag my name before the public ... I do most strongly object to my name being made use of in the way it has been. It would be bad enough if the statements made by 'Argus' were true but they are a tissue of most disgraceful falsehoods written, I suppose to injure me in the eyes of the public. Why should I and this parish be selected for his unjust and untrue comments when the rent charge of my three nieghbouring parishes Warlingham, Coulsdon and Beddington all exceed mine in value and which is not half what he states it to be ... Now I must emphatically declare that not a single penny was paid either by me, or my father, or anyone connected with me to the patron of this living in order to place me in the position which I now hold ... I was presented to this living by the patron, whom I had known from boyhood ... I am not the only person who has to complain of your anonymous correspondent's personal comments and I have often heard it remarked that what he writes is of the most offensive. At all events there ought to be some guarantee that what he writes is true and not false. I have the honour to remain, Your obedient Servant, John Randolph, Sanderstead Rectory, January 8th, 1877'

The younger John Randolph was a sporting man and had played county cricket. As Rector and personal friend of the Squire, he was able to participate in the hunting and shooting activities that the Squire's estate was able to provide. However in later life he suffered ill-health which left him depressed. Probably as a result, he took his own life by shooting himself in the mouth with a pistol early one morning in July 1881. At the coroner's inquest, held in the Sanderstead Board School, the jury of local men quickly decided that their Rector had taken his own life while of unsound mind. The parish thus was able to give him a Christian burial in his own churchyard in a grave alongside his father.

There was no provision for nonconformists in Sanderstead, their nearest place of worship being the Methodist chapel in Warlingham.

The Village Population

The population of Sanderstead was the same in 1861 as it had been in 1801. Because the Squire owned the land which in turn was worked by a small number of his tenants, he could control the number of cottages on the estate, and so was able to exercise control over the number of residents in the village. In this way the resident population was restricted to the number of people for whom there was work, and few could stay if they had none. This was important as far as the Squire and his substantial tenants were concerned, since at that time financial assistance to the poor was paid from the rates levied on property in the parish.

Table 1 below shows the population of the parish through the 19th century and Table 2 shows the number of houses, occupied and vacant at different times. Changes in the population are clearly mirrored by changes in the number of dwellings. The apparently high population figure for 1841 is misleading. The resident population

Thought to be Borough Farm, *c.*1880

Old Fox Path, *c.*1900

A HISTORY OF SANDERSTEAD

was 219, and the remainder comprised 45 itinerants that the enumerator counted despite the fact that they had left the parish before he could interview them. He recorded that 17 of the itinerants had spent census night in barns, sheds and the like, and described them as being 'mostly Irish in search of Haying', casual work which would have been in demand in early June when this census was taken. The other 28 he described as Gypsies living in tents or the open air.

Table 1   The population of Sanderstead

	Males	Females	Total
1801	113	91	204
1811	104	81	185
1821	101	88	189
1831	119	123	242
1841	136	128	264
1851	123	112	235
1861	110	96	206
1871	143	124	267
1881	200	182	382
1891	207	202	409
1901*	492	509	1001

Table 2   The number of dwellings in the parish

	Occupied	Uninhabited	Building	Total
1801	33	1	0	34
1811	31	0	0	31
1821	31	2	0	33
1831	34	1	0	35
1841	34	0	0	34
1851	38	0	0	38
1861	41	0	0	41
1871	54	6	0	60
1881	100	3	2	105
1891	96	9	0	105
1901*	203	4	8	215

* Including Selsdon

THE 19TH CENTURY – AN ESTATE VILLAGE

There was no overall addition to the total number of houses in the parish during the first 40 years of the century, and the number of dwellings matched the population of the village. In 1841, the census enumerator thought it surprising that there were no houses unoccupied or being built in the parish, and wrote a note on his return confirming that this was in fact the case. During the middle years of the century there was some modest development and several groups of cottages were built for workers employed on the estate farms. Some of these new houses replaced older dwellings, as for example a group of five opposite 'The White House'. These five dwellings may originally have been part of the outhouses of a larger house, 'Sanderstead Place', demolished some 50 years earlier. The new cottages were built in the style made fashionable by the Prince of Wales and were decorated with the Atwood 'Axe-in-Hand' crest.

Employment in the village was almost entirely connected with agriculture or with the services needed at the large houses. Table 3 gives a breakdown of the main occupations. The parish consisted of agricultural labourers, shepherds, carters, gardeners and gamekeepers, though the proportion of households primarily engaged in agriculture declined over the century. There was also a blacksmith and a wheelwright, and various indoor and outdoor domestic servants, both male and female. There was usually a young woman in the village who earned a living as a dressmaker and – towards the end of the century – some women who took in laundry. It is also clear from the Census that children as young as 10 or 11 were often employed.

Table 3 Principle occupation of householders

	Agriculture	Trades & handicrafts	Other
1801	-	-	-
1811	18	4	9
1821	23	4	4
1831	27	2	11
1841	23	4	10
1851	39	4	12
1861	20	6	16
1871	20	7	21
1881	40	16	14
1891	No comparable figures available		
1901	No comparable figures available		

In the final quarter of the century the population increased, and with it the number of houses in the village. These were mainly at the northern end of the parish. A number of large houses had been built near the newly opened Sanderstead railway station, and these were occupied by professional people who worked in Croydon and London. There was also a number of cottages which were occupied mainly by labourers and artisans who worked in the new shoemaking industry of South Croydon. The land that was developed in this way had not been owned by the Wigsells but by the Croydon charities.

The number of people living in Sanderstead may have changed little, but the individuals living there changed frequently. This was particularly so in the case of agricultural workers and both male and female domestic servants. Typically only a quarter of the residents included in one census had been there 10 years previously, and even fewer as the century passed. Furthermore, these itinerant workers did not come from nearby parishes as might be expected. Instead – as Table 4 shows – many had come from more distant parts of Surrey or even much further afield, and this was increasingly so as the century progressed.

Table 4 Places of origin of residents of working age (over 14 years)

	1851 %	1881 %
Sanderstead	17	3
an adjacent parish (i.e. 5km)	21	13
a day's walk of Sanderstead (i.e. 20km)	11	13
the rest of South East England	32	35
the rest of the country	19	36

Rarely was more than one branch of a family resident in the parish at the same time. Only one person, George Groves, an agricultural labourer, appeared in every census of Sanderstead from 1841 to 1891, and he had been born in Brighton.

Those who showed any stability were the few parish tradesmen such as the Bex family, who were wheelwrights and carpenters, and the Saker family, brickmakers and bricklayers, who were present throughout much of the century. So too were the Leppards. William Saker was a local man but even he had been born in Warlingham not Sanderstead. James Bex came from Sussex. Other carpenters and blacksmiths were employed in the village for short periods of time but put down no roots and soon moved on.

Farming

The Parish was not of prime agricultural land but, apart from some 370 acres of woodland, it was extensively farmed. Robert Russell of Borough Farm passed his tenancy on to his son, also Robert, but this was the only occasion in the late 18th or 19th centuries when this happened. Towards the end of the century, as farms became vacant, the Arkwrights, then the squires, took the management into their own hands, for example at White House Farm Samuel Cowdrey was appointed bailiff. A manager was appointed to run Borough Farm.

In 1843, at the time of the commutation of the Tithes, almost 70% of the land was used for arable farming and only 13% for pasture. The most important arable crop was oats but this was a low value product. A small amount of barley and even less wheat was grown. At that time, oats fetched only 2s.9d a bushel and barley 4s.0d a bushel, while wheat sold for 7s. a bushel. These prices were lower than they had been earlier in the century because of the shortages resulting from the Napoleonic Wars despite the protection from overseas competition given to farmers by the Corn Laws. These laws were repealed in 1846, and agricultural prosperity continued to decline throughout the rest of the century in the face of increasing cheap imports from abroad.

At the start of the 19th century, woodlands accounted for nearly a fifth of the parish, little different from now. At that time woodlands here in Sanderstead, as elsewhere, were a valuable local resource providing timber for the local community for fuel, tools and building. The deposits of clay-with-flints above the chalk were a source of clay for brick-making and the chalk itself a source for marling the fields. As the century progressed these local resources were undercut by cheap imported timber, the advent of machine-made bricks and the increasing use of coal for fuel, all of which became readily available with the development of the railways.

As the economic importance of the woodlands declined, the recreational use increased and greater importance was attached to them as game reserves. The game available, according to clauses in various leases, included wildfowl, hares and rabbits. Sanderstead was also renowned for its hunting pack of Blue-mottle Harriers. The

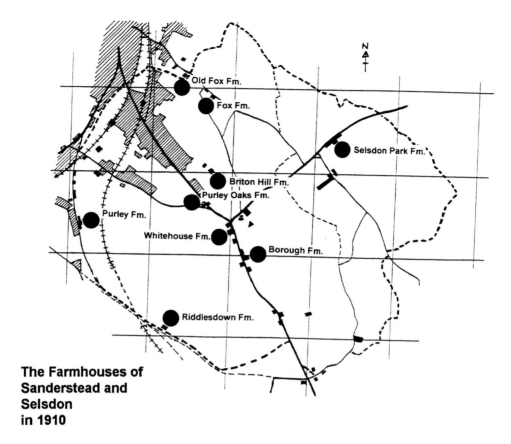

**The Farmhouses of
Sanderstead and
Selsdon
in 1910**

Fox Farm in 1997

150 acres of King's Wood, formerly known as Sanderstead Woods, which extends from the present Lime Meadow Avenue to the parish boundary at Hamsey Green, was the main area converted into a game reserve with improved facilities for shooting. A series of rides were cut through the wood dividing it into seven or eight acre blocks. Four distinctive conifers were planted at each of the intersections of the rides so that the junctions could be seen and so hopefully prevent shooting accidents as people crossed them. A few of these conifers remain. A cottage was provided in the wood for a gamekeeper in 1870 and it is still occupied.

Education

Sanderstead had a school from an early date – at least from before 1831. The school was founded by the Squire and the Rector for the parish children and like much public education at this time with the spiritual needs of the poor in mind by enabling them to read the Bible rather than to improve their social status. In the 1820s and 30s, the school was held in an unidentified house in the village, but we know it was later housed in one of a group of old cottages opposite White House Farm and that the school mistress in 1841 was Susannah Newman, wife of one of the servants at 'Sanderstead Court'.

Ten years later, after the old cottages were demolished, the school moved to one of the outbuildings of the Rectory. The teacher, who also lived there, was a young woman, Miss Ellen Maria Coombe. She also acted as the village postmistress – perhaps because she was one of the few adult residents able to read. In 1875 a School Board was formed under the Chairmanship of the Rector, with Samuel Cowdrey – the Squire's estate manager – as its clerk. This Board was responsible for building and operating a new purpose-built school and schoolteacher's house. It was built for 75 pupils, but the average attendance then was only about 40 and the school was not used to its full capacity until the 20th century. At the time of the move to the new school building, the schoolmistress was Miss Mary Jane Baggs and she was helped by a series of assistant mistresses. The 1875 school building is now used as the dining hall for the Gresham School, the main buildings of which lie behind it.

(See also Chapter 12)

Shops

During the 19th century there was rarely more than one shop at a time in Sanderstead. In 1841 Eliza Nichols, then aged 86, ran a general store. As the Churchwarden's accounts book suggests, she may well have been a regular supplier of brooms and other necessities to the church for a number of years before that. The following year, the accounts show that James Dudley, her son-in-law, was supplying the Church and certainly by 1851 he was running a grocery and baker's shop which he and later his widow continued to do until she died in 1873. This shop was originally two cottages and still exists next to Gresham School. James Dudley rented his shop on a short lease, presumably from the Squire, Atwood Wigsell, but he also owned a barn in the village for storing his flour. In 1861, James Brook combined a chandler's shop with blacksmithing.

By 1878, the shop was run by the Frosels. Trade directories of the period give James Frosel as the shopkeeper but the 1881 census shows him to be an agricultural worker on the Arkwright estate. The census gives no occupation for his wife, Ann, but she is believed to have run the shop at this time. Ann was clearly quite a character, smoking a pipe in public! In the 1891 census James Frosel was described as the grocer, and the Frosels had taken over the post office duties from the schoolmistress. They also sold beer, wines and spirits, which were for consumption off the premises only, no public houses being allowed in the village.

By 1891, the situation had changed dramatically, with the new developments at the north of the parish where there were now a number of shops – a grocer, greengrocer and various general dealers, one of whom had formerly been a policeman stationed in the village.

(See also Chapter 14)

Law and Order

Sanderstead employed a parish constable from about 1838. This appointment was held on a part-time basis by George Botley at a salary of £2.2s.0d a year, paid by the churchwardens from parish funds. Botley continued his work as an agricultural labourer during the rest of his time. A small Metropolitan Police post or 'manor' was established in Sanderstead from before 1851. This was an outstation of the police division based at Croydon. Botley, however, seems to have continued as the parish constable after this station opened but at a reduced salary of £1.1s.0d a year.

The Sanderstead Metropolitan Police Station fronted the Limpsfield Road near Hamsey Green and consisted of a small lock-up, a stable and living quarters for married officers, on an acre of land. There were usually two or three policemen attached to the station, sometimes including a police sergeant. The station served a wide area and covered Warlingham, Chelsham, Whyteleafe and Kenley as well as Sanderstead. One officer who served there for many years was Benjamin Beeson, a veteran of the Charge of the Light Brigade in the Crimean War. He served as a mounted policeman, carrying out his duties until he retired aged 62 in 1892. He died in 1908 and was given a hero's funeral. His grave is in Sanderstead churchyard.

Roads, Railways and other Communications.

The main road through the village, now the Limpsfield Road had fallen into disrepair, in part at least because of the increase in wheeled traffic during the 18th century, but also because the parishes through which it passed had neglected their duties to maintain it. In 1813, this road was turnpiked.

Sanderstead Road – a painting by J.B.James c.1900 *Courtesy of Croydon Library*

Roads were relatively no less hazardous then than they are now. In April 1881 Henry Heritage – a carter – was killed when he slipped under the wheels of his own cart, and while the Coroner's court was considering his death, another road accident happened nearby. Six year old Willie Bex, the son of James Bex the village carpenter and wheelwright, was killed when he fell from the cart driven by his 17-year old elder brother, Walter, and landed under the wheels of another cart laden with sand being driven by William Harbour of Warlingham. The Coroner, when he had finished the inquest on Henry Heritage, immediately conducted the inquest into the death of young Willie Bex.

This was never a busy road, but unlike many other turnpikes its tolls would not have been significantly affected by the expansion of the railways since no railway competed directly with it. The road remained without a tarmacadam surface until long after the end of the century.

Sanderstead was on the daily mail run from Croydon through Warlingham to other nearby parishes. The mail was exempt from turnpike tolls. The mounted postman delivered letters for the residents of the parish to the schoolmistress early in the morning and, until the first pillar post box was installed in about 1870, picked up outgoing letters on his return in the afternoon. Later, there were two deliveries and several collections a day, even on Sundays. By the end of the century money orders could be purchased at Sanderstead but could only be cashed in Warlingham. Sanderstead Station was the nearest telegraph office.

The main London and Brighton Railway Company railway line skirted the western edge of the parish. There was no station near the village, and the railway seems to have had no noticeable effect on it. No doubt until they became used to them, the new steam engines would have frightened horses and cattle in the fields near the track especially at Purley Oaks Farm and 'Purley Bury House', and sparks from the engines would have been a regular hazard for ripening crops in nearby fields.

In 1884 another railway was built at the north end of the parish with a station at Sanderstead. Being a long way from the centre, it probably did not affect village life very much, but it did lead to the housing development described in the next chapter.

SOURCES

All Saints' Parish Records and Memorials

Atwood Family Wills and leases (originally held by Messrs. Hatton, Asplin,
    Jewers & Glenny - Solicitors, Grays, Essex)

Census for Sanderstead 1841, 1851, 1861, 1871, 1881, 1891

Ecclesiastical Census 1851

Land Tax Returns for Sanderstead - 1781 to 1793

PACKHAM, R. (1986) 'The Tragedy of a Sanderstead Rector', Bourne Society *Local History Records* 25

Return of the Owners of Land 1873 - Surrey

Sanderstead Churchwardens' Account Book

Tithe Apportionment for Sanderstead - 1843

Trade Directories for Surrey - various 1851 to 1899

Will of Atwood Dalton Wigsell

Chapter 7

Early Expansion

researched by Bob Adams, Vernon Briggs and Ted Frith

At the end of the 19th century and for the first few years of the 20th there was little change in the pattern of life in the old village. It retained its quiet rural character and was largely governed by the Lord of the Manor, the last hereditary owner of the title being Captain Esme Wigsell Arkwright.

Prior to the establishment of the railway there was no apparent demand for new houses or roads. The population was still small – 1001, including Selsdon, in the Census of 1901. The accelerating development in rail and road transport described more fully in chapter 13 was however bound to have an effect in the long run, as the old order changed 'yielding place to new'. These changes had already been foreseen well before the end of the 19th century, and preparations had already begun to modernise living standards, expand local government and plan for the future.

The commercial development of the lands that comprised the Wigsell estates was envisaged from at least the 1870s, since Atwood Dalton Wigsell gave his executors powers to spend money on developing the estate land – a power that was probably first used in the Coulsdon area, but by the turn of the century had been applied to Sanderstead too. An extract from his will reads 'by laying out such money in the formation of roads, sewers and other improvements as shall be thought adequate for the interests therein ....'

Local Government

Other changes initiated before the end of the 19th century were those affecting local government. Under the Public Health Act of 1875, the Croydon Rural Sanitary Authority was set up to regulate health, sewerage, building and highway matters in the parishes surrounding Croydon. In the first report of the Authority in 1878 the acreage of Sanderstead was given as 2661, the population (in 1871) as 267, and the rateable value £6649. The first member of the Authority to represent Sanderstead was the Revd. John Randolph, who was succeeded after his death by Thomas Chandler of Purley Oaks Farm and then – from 1883-1891 – by Thomas Langford, who was the tenant farmer at Selsdon Park Farm.

The Medical Officer of Health for the Coulsdon, Sanderstead and Addington District reported each year on the number and causes of deaths. In 1883 a navvy was killed in an accident involving a railway engine, while in 1888 there was an outbreak of diphtheria in Selsdon, and three young children died. In June 1891 an outbreak of typhoid fever occurred in the area, and measles was prevalent in October 1892. In 1893 two cottages at Paddy's Bottom, Sanderstead, were condemned as being unfit for human habitation.

In 1894 the Sanitary Authority was replaced by Croydon Rural District Council and this continued until the formation of Coulsdon & Purley Urban District Council in 1915. For the whole of this period the councillor for Sanderstead was an architect, James Williams, of Beechwood Road.

The Parish Councils Act of 1894 brought parish councils into being, and details of the elections for the first of these, held in December 1894, were reported in the *Croydon Advertiser* but unfortunately those for Sanderstead were not included. We do however have the names of 33 Sanderstead residents who served as parish councillors between 1895 and 1915.

1895	James Williams	1904	Percy Chant
	William Wilson		Charles Robert Shaw Stewart
	Thomas Dulake		John William Straughan
	Bertram David Brand	1907	Bernard Mervyn Drake
	William Stevens		Charles Stewart Austin
	George Clinging		Henry Hooper
	Charles Fielder		Henry Oswald Smith
	Henry Landon Maud		John Lewis Verne
1897	Alfred Carpenter	1908	George Edgell Mills
1898	Frederick Lynche Blosse	1910	George Dudley Brown
1899	Samuel Bowman		Harry North
	Henry Thomas Muggeridge	1911	William Saunders
1901	John Broadbridge	1913	John Martin Burtenshaw
	Walter James Beall		Ernest Alfred Cross
	Wickham Noakes		Herbert Joseph Glassborow
	James John Davies	1914	Jasper Henry Edmund Nicolls
			William John Woolrich

(From the Declaration of Acceptance Register).

Parish councillors between 1895 and 1915.

In the years before World War I, the changes initiated by the developments in transport, education and trade at the end of the 19th century continued to move slowly forward; neither was Sanderstead immune from the political upheavals that were beginning to erupt, with the demand for greater franchise and for votes for women. There was more unemployment than hitherto, and in 1904 the Croydon Poor Law Guardians decided to establish a Poor Law Station in Sanderstead; a site for it was purchased in Sanderstead Road for £360. The building itself cost £915 and was completed the following year. Sanderstead paid £1182 – almost all of the cost – and Samuel Cowdrey at 'The White House' was the first Assistant Overseer.

The Poor Law Station in Sanderstead Road

(Photographed in 1998)

Mayfield Road at the turn of the century and (below) in 1997

In 1904 the number of persons receiving aid was seven. There were also casual vagrants who were permitted to stay overnight before travelling on for a 'fee' of:

Males:	Stonebreaking – 10 cwt in 2" pieces
Females:	9 hours labour in the washhouse.

Health care was private, and those who could not afford it had to resort to collecting a 'pass' from Queens Road, Croydon, which enabled them to be helped and prescribed for at the local Poor Law Union Office. From the 1891 Census it appears that there were no resident doctors in Sanderstead.

The other duties of the resident administrator were:

> Registration of births, marriages and deaths
>
> Arranging for the inpatient care of lunatics
>
> Accommodation of deserted wives and children
>
> Lying-in accommodation at the Hospital in Mayday Road
>
> Collecting dues for the upkeep of these from relatives

There was a medical examination room and changing cubicles for each sex on either side of the Poor Law Station. The Medical Officer in 1905 was Doctor Pollack who lived in Warlingham. He received a retainer of £50 a year plus medical fees, and patients came from a catchment area of Sanderstead, Selsdon, Purley and Warlingham.

Utilities and Services

Gas – There were also important developments in the provision of utilities and services. In 1820 Mr. Overton had opened a gas works in Surrey Street and supplied gas to Croydon from 1820-1847. His business was then taken over by the Croydon Commercial Gas and Coke Company, incorporated as a company limited by shares under Act of Parliament. In streets through which a gas main ran the gas could be used to provide street lighting on terms agreed with the Council. This supply was at first restricted to the town and parish of Croydon but a further Act of Parliament in 1866 empowered the Company to increase its capital and extend its area of operation to include Addington, Beddington, Coulsdon and Sanderstead. It also gave the Company power to develop the Waddon Gas Works. The maximum price for the gas was prescribed by statute at 5s. per 1000 cu.ft. The railway stations of Caterham Junction (now Purley), Kenley and Warlingham (now Whyteleafe South) were the first to be supplied – the last in 1873 – and by 1908 this gas was made available to Sanderstead, but there were at first only three street lamps – one at Sanderstead Station near the bridge, one at the top of Sanderstead Hill by the pond, and one at the junction of Sanderstead Road and Purley Downs Road. Written on the glass of these gas lamps was the location of the nearest fire alarm.

Water – Water supplies came at first from wells – the parish church, every farm, and many of the houses and cottages had their own well. However, at the close of the 19th century the estate had its own water supply coming from the Kenley Water Works pumping station near the cross-roads at Purley. The water was pumped across the fields and there was at least one trough filled from a standard which tapped the main as it passed near Riddlesdown. There was also a reservoir on the high ground of Sanderstead Plantation opposite the church, and water could thence be fed to the whole village. In March 1876 the newly built school was quoted 2s. 6d. per 1000 gallons for a metered supply. Annual rent for the meter was 18s. 0d. payable in advance. In 1881 the Kenley Water Works Company merged with the Caterham Spring Water Company to form the East Surrey Water Company, which as the Sutton and East Surrey Water Company is still the local supplier today.

Pumping water outside the village school – *ca.* 1906

Housing Development

One of the earliest estates of houses to be built in Sanderstead was on land between Purley Oaks and Sanderstead Stations. The fields of Purley Oaks Farm, between the two railway lines, were offered for auction in 1903, and by 1905 the first houses were occupied. There were certain conditions attached to the sale to ensure that the dwellings could only be bought by professional people, and the building on each plot had to cost a minimum of £700, exclusive of outbuildings and fences. This caused homes of very high standard for the period to be built and the following detailed description of a pair of houses at 1 and 3 Penwortham Road illustrates this well:

'The rooms designed for us by the owners and their family were large, lofty and elaborately decorated with a central corbel. The skirting boards were 12 inches high and carved. There were cast-iron fireplaces with wooden surrounds in all the rooms including the entrance hall and bell-pulls featured prominently by the side of the fireplaces. There was even one in the bathroom, and of course by the front and back doors.

By contrast, the quarters of the live-in maid or housekeeper were much humbler, and she was expected to spend all her day about the house, on call at any time, summoned by bells which registered on a number board above the kitchen door. There was a built-in Welsh dresser, a worktop under the window and a solid-fuel cooking range opposite. Behind this was the scullery, a smaller austere room with a quarry-tiled floor, a shallow Belfast sink with a cold water tap on the wall above. A stove for heating water stood in one corner. The walls of the scullery were lime-washed and there was only one small window by the sink to give natural light or ventilation. By the side of this window was the back door or tradesmen's entrance which also led to an outside toilet for the servant's use. Leading out of the scullery was a pantry with built-in shelves on either side, and a fuel store which was filled from the outside.

The housekeeper's bedroom, for she slept 'on the job', was a small plainly decorated room at the back of the house, with a door that was both narrower and lower than any other in the house.'

1-3 Penwortham Road

Live-in maids and other domestic servants were the norm for these and later houses, and a tradesmen's entrance at the side or rear of the house was essential. Great attention was paid to the materials used in building these houses, which had 9" x 3" joists, 6" x 2" rafters, solid oak window sills, and ¼" plate glass glazing, very often with all the edges bevelled. The fanlights were glazed with coloured leaded glass and the very high ceilings in the main rooms often had elaborate plasterwork.

One of the selling points claimed by the estate agents for these houses was the nearness to the railway, and this was considered to be the transport of the future! Even though the first motor cars had already arrived on Britain's roads, no one foresaw how dominant they would prove to be before the century was ended, and as today's purchasers of these houses know to their cost, no provision was made for garages.

SOURCES

Croydon Local Studies Library

Croydon Advertiser

Chapter 8

The Great War 1914 – 1918

by Roger Packham

In considering the events of World War I in the small parish of Sanderstead, it is easy to assume that, unlike the 1939-45 conflict, life probably continued in much the same way as in peacetime – except for the shocks sustained on receipt of bad news from the western front. A search of the local newspapers quickly dispels this view, and the modest population was very much involved in some tremendously hard work in assisting the war effort. The Sanderstead Special Constabulary was formed within a few days of the outbreak of war and at one time numbered 143. From the 'Specials' 118 joined the forces, and as late as February 1919 there were still 91 Special Constables. Chief Inspector Kirkman won much acclaim for his unwavering zeal in the execution of his duties.

With so many of their menfolk enlisted in the armed forces, women took over many of the men's jobs and this had considerable long-term social effects, giving women a greater say in affairs and more freedom, and not least led to great changes in women's fashions. The names recorded on Sanderstead war memorial in the grounds of All Saints' parish church show that few families escaped tragedy. 67 men lost their lives out of a total population of under 1000, accounting for probably 25 - 30% of the eligible manpower.

War Memorial Sanderstead .Surrey.

Home Front in Sanderstead

Away from the activities of the Special Constabulary, the gentry of Sanderstead organised themselves into various committees designed to aid specific aspects of the war effort. The following extracts from local newspapers convey something of the desire to help, and at different times groups were set up for Belgian Refugees, War Relief Fund, United Workers, Purley Oaks Allotment Holders and a Sanderstead Flat for a disabled serviceman in Fulham. The reports also include some contemporary news items concerning Lights Out, Absenteeism and Exemption from Fighting —

Boy Scouts outside the school in 1914 – Scouts contributed greatly to the war effort

Belgian Refugee Committee

January 1915 – The Committee for the Parish of Sanderstead has issued a report. It is under the presidency of Capt. A. Carpenter (sen) RN, DSO and includes Lady Bailey, Mrs. Bartlett, Mrs. Carter, Mrs. Harrison, Mrs. Jacques, Mrs. Prideaux, Mrs. Tomalin, Revd. A. Watson-Smyth MA, Mr. S. Bowman.

A House Sub-committee was formed for housing and maintaining the Belgian Refugees with Mrs. Harrison and Mrs. Sargeant acting as chairman and hon. secretary. Mr. G. Idiens has placed at the disposal of the committee his residence – 'Hurst Bank', Upper Selsdon Road – and Doctors Oswald Smith and Everington have kindly promised free attendance. The East Surrey Water Co. has agreed to supply water free of charge until 25th March; gifts of coal have been made by Lady Bailey and Messrs. Hall & Co, Messrs Dyson & Son have lent an excellent piano free of charge and Mr. & Mrs. Idiens will allow the free use of the electric light apparatus. Local tradesmen have also contributed to the fund by liberal reductions to their charges.

November 1915 – The first party of Belgian Refugees arrived on 9th November. The number of guests varies but it is now 27. The entire housework is done by the refugees but the sub-committee takes turns to cook the dinner. A resident housekeeper has been appointed to relieve the sub-committee. The committee has promised to continue the maintenance of 'Hurst Bank' but would like to extend help to the refugees by boarding-out families in the parish.

THE GREAT WAR 1914 – 1918

War Relief Fund

January 1915 – A report was issued by Mr. S. Bowman, chairman of the War Relief Fund for the parish of Sanderstead: about 80 Sanderstead residents were now serving in HM Forces; 634 garments have now been made and sent to the Red Cross Society; Mrs. Tomalin, 'Hazel Glen', Sanderstead Road, deals with applications for District Medical Relief which are then forwarded to Revd. Watson-Smyth, the Parsonage, Purley Oaks Road. The subscriptions received amount to £1021 and this has been allocated to the Prince of Wales National Relief Fund, Sailors' and Soldiers' Families Associations and local Red Cross Emergency Fund. Mrs. Woolrich of 'Friston', Beechwood Road, will be glad to receive further subscriptions to the national fund – the calls upon which are very heavy.

Flowers for Daddy

July 1915 – The following note, forwarded by an Old Whitgiftian to his father at Sanderstead brings out in striking fashion the poignant pathos of the war. The soldier, speaking of the battle of Festubert, says: 'The only men from our battalion who came to actual grips with the enemy were ten in bombers. Only two of these returned. Pinned to the little wooden cross of a Captain's grave is a letter in a child's straggling writing, with some flowers: "I hope you will like these flowers Daddy". The flowers and the message came too late'.

The Sanderstead Musical Society

April 1916 – The Sanderstead Musical Society gave a Russian Musical concert, rich and rare, in aid of the Addington Park War Hospital, at the small Public Hall, Croydon. The programme included many fine expositions of the works of some of the most prominent Russian composers, including Tchaikowsky, Glazunow, Arensky and Moussorgsky. Perhaps none gave one a better idea of the Russian spirit than the quaint and dreamy folk songs and the plaintive mighty agonising 'Russia's Prayer' that made visible the Teuton masses, countless, ruthless, threatening hordes and ended with the cry of the child on the world's great altar stairs of the mighty steppes – 'God Save our Russia'.

United Workers – How we can all help in the War

April 1916 – Under the auspices of the above organisation, a drawing room meeting was held at 'Linnaea', Sanderstead, by kind invitation of Mrs. Wettern. The aim of the United Workers' movement is to impress upon us all the essential fact that the success in the war depends upon financial endurance of the allies and to make it more generally recognised how urgent and vital the matter is and how much depends upon what the individual does with his own resources... It was decided to establish a War Savings Bank in Sanderstead and to follow up the meeting with a public evening meeting.

Sanderstead Rifle Club

May 1916 – The Rifle Club held its annual meeting at 'The Range', Mayfield Road, with Mr. Clement Paul in the chair. It was important for every man to learn to shoot now that the Compulsion Bill is becoming law.

Wounded Heroes at 'Sanderstead Court'

July 1916 – by courtesy of Mr. & Mrs Edward Moreton. Mr. & Mrs. Moreton have placed their picturesque residence, with its spacious lawns, its beautiful flower gardens, its well-stocked kitchen garden and its rows of glasshouses at the disposal of some 80 wounded soldiers from some of the hospitals in London... as so many of them truly remarked, it was like heaven. And so it was, for these war-scarred warriors, many of whom came from faraway Australia and were making their first acquaintance with a real old English garden... They had been brought by the Corporation of London Motor Volunteers from Mile End, Lewisham and Dulwich... There was an unlimited supply of cigarettes and the soldiers indulged themselves in bowls, tennis, quoits and a novel automatic figure, representing the Kaiser, who raised his arms in token of surrender when struck by a missile thrown by the more athletic and those in a more advanced stage of recovery. Tea was served on the lawn with plenty of fruit, sandwiches and all sorts of cake. Musical entertainment followed and then each was presented with a bunch of flowers for going back.

For many months now, Mr. & Mrs. Moreton have turned one of the large rooms at their house, opening onto the lawn and facing as lovely a stretch of country as can be found in England, into a special ward for convalescent members of the Royal Navy... Those who feel that they want to give an outing during the summer weather to our men in hospital should communicate with Mr. Alder, 'Montrose', Hook Hill or Mrs. Robinson, 89 Mayfield Road.

Purley Oaks Allotment Holders' Association

September 1916 – A well attended meeting was held at 'The Gatehouse', Kendall Avenue South, Sanderstead on Saturday evening with Coun. Cross in the chair, when it was resolved to form the above association for mutual exchange of experience, co-operative purchase of seeds and kindred purposes. It was resolved to ask Mr. Kerly, Chairman of the Purley & Coulsdon UDC to become President.

Garden Fete and Pastoral Play

July 1916 – A fete was held in the grounds of 'Red Gables', 'The Coppice' and 'Beech Corner', Beech Avenue, Sanderstead, in aid of the Sanderstead Flat, in the War Seals Mansion, Fulham, for Disabled Married Servicemen...This was one of the most elaborate of high class entertainments, most perfectly arranged including an orchestra, that Sanderstead has seen for many days and its promoters may well be proud of their efforts in a noble cause.

Sanderstead Memorial Hall – photographed in 1997

Purley Tribunal

August 1916 – Mr. H.J. Bounder of Sanderstead feels that he ought to appeal against being called up. He has a wife and five children and will be 40 in December. Meanwhile he is carrying on an ironmonger's business in Godstone Road, Kenley, for a very small salary. The Tribunal in spite of these facts, rules that there is no case for exemption and that he will get a good allowance.

Lights of Sanderstead

August 1917 – At Croydon County Bench, Thrale Jell of 'Hayling', Beechwood Road, Sanderstead, was summoned for disobeying blackout regulations. Edward Boston, a Sanderstead 'Special' said that at 11.15 p.m. he and another Special saw the light at the side of the house. When they rang at the door, the light immediately went out. Defendant said the light was turned up for half a second while he rinsed his hands. Boston was officious – very gruff indeed. Called back to the bench, Boston denied this. Jell: 'Well, according to the rules of the Special Constabulary, it is part of your duty to be respectful and courteous to people'. Another Special said it was four minutes before the door was answered. Chief Inspector Lovie said the defendant had caused a great deal of trouble: he had pooh-poohed the idea of anyone going to his house about the lights and had received five warnings. There had been a great deal of talk among residents. Fined 20s.

Boys arrested in Sanderstead

December 1917 – William Stammers and Albert Reeves, both 16, were arrested in Sanderstead and came before the Croydon bench charged with being absentees from a reserve training battalion of East Surreys. Stammers said it was because they did not get enough to eat. Mrs. Reeves said steps had been taken to get her son released because he was under age: she asserted that he was medically unfit. The boys were handed over to military custody.

Sanderstead War Savings Association

January 1919 – The total amount of money raised was £117,769.

The Hero of Zeebrugge – Capt. A F B Carpenter VC (1881-1955)

Captain Alfred Francis Blakeney Carpenter, son and grandson of distinguished naval officers, was the hero of Zeebrugge, where he commanded HMS *Vindictive* during the attack on 23rd April 1918 and for which he won the Victoria Cross, the Croix de Guerre and was created an Officer of the Legion of Honour. He later wrote *The Battle of Zeebrugge* (1921) following a lecture tour of Canada and the United States. During World War I, his father (also Captain Alfred Carpenter) lived at 'The Red House', Sanderstead, and was no doubt the proud parent when the hero returned home in May, 1918. The local newspaper reported:

'Residents of Sanderstead (at the invitation of Mr. & Mrs. Bowman) met at 'Fairmount', Glossop Road, on Wednesday evening for the purpose of welcoming Capt. A F B Carpenter, the hero of Zeebrugge. The meeting was of a semi-private nature and owing to the limited accommodation, was confined to relatives and friends of the family and friends of Captain A Carpenter, the father of the hero. There were present, in addition, Sir Arthur Spurgeon, Chairman of the County bench and Mr. Kerly, Chairman of the District Council. The Revd. W. Brooke Rickards, Rector of the Parish, in a welcoming speech, voiced the admiration of Sanderstead for the very brave part which Captain Carpenter took in the attack of Zeebrugge and offered warm congratulations to the father.

Capt. A F B Carpenter in reply, gave some most interesting particulars of the adventure. With the usual modesty attached to men in the Navy, he protested that the successful carrying out of the enterprise was just a matter of good fortune as far as he was concerned and paid a very high tribute of praise to the officers and men associated with him... With a view to further commemorating Capt. Carpenter's exploits, arrangements are being made for his portrait to be painted by an eminent Royal Academician, who has very kindly undertaken the task on the understanding that any fee paid to him shall be passed onto the Red Cross Fund. It is intended that the portrait, when painted, shall be presented to Capt. Alfred Carpenter, sen., as a token of this parish's warm recognition of his son's bravery and also as an expression of the great regard which is felt for the father.'

Sanderstead Heroes

It is disappointing not to find more details of the Sanderstead soldiers – especially the fallen – in the local newspapers, and there is no record of a contemporary parish magazine, which might have contained such information. There is thus an opportunity for further research, but below are included some of the few published details—

CARTER, Capt. Malcolm Russell – E. Surrey Regiment, second son of Mr. & Mrs. Henry Carter of 'Steep', Beech Avenue, Sanderstead, was reported killed in action. Aged 24. (April 1918)

CHATTERTON, Second-Lieut. Harold M N – Queens, Royal W. Surrey Regiment, was killed by gas poisoning. He was the only son of Mr. & Mrs. Chatterton of Sanderstead. There will be a memorial service at St. Paul's Presbyterian Church, South Croydon, today. (June 1916)

COWDREY, Corporal Basil of the Queens, is the eldest son of Mr. & Mrs. Cowdrey of Edgar Road, Sanderstead. He joined the Army in 1914 when he was 15 years old and was sent on active service last January. He has been through many engagements and finally distinguished himself with three comrades by holding a post at Meteran for three days without cessation until reinforcements came ... For this conspicuous bravery he was highly commended and was given the Military Medal. He is now on leave pending a commission in the RAF. (July 1918)

DAVIES, H H of Sanderstead, 6156 Royal Sussex Regiment, killed. (Sept. 1917)

DAVIES, Captain James Gordon - 10th (1st Rhondda), the Welsh Regiment, was killed in France on 9th February. He was the only son of Mr. & Mrs. J.J. Davies of 'Gwynnescote', Hove Park, Hove and late of Sanderstead Hill. (February 1916)

DYSON, Captain J. Gordon – 1st Royal Berkshire Regiment, has been appointed fire inspector to the RAF for the Midland District. Capt. Dyson was Chief of the Sanderstead Fire Brigade when the war broke out. (December 1918)

EKINS, Lieutenant Franklin George (Barney) of 1st Battalion, Royal Irish Regiment died from septic pneumonia at the Military Hospital, Cherbourg, aged 22. He was from Sheffield and was the nephew of Mr. W. Mitchison, Broomhall Road, Sanderstead. (February 1919)

GATLAND, Private Ernest was killed on 3rd November. He was born in Sanderstead Road, Croydon and his parents live in Rolleston Road. (December 1917)

HAMMOND, Captain Hugh Jerrold – Gloucestershire Regiment, late 1st Royal Warwicks Regiment, was reported killed on 28th March, aged 26. He was the elder son of Mr. & Mrs. Hammond of 'St. Olave's', Mayfield Road, Sanderstead. (April 1918)

HARRISON, Lieutenant-Colonel Edward Frank, CMG – Royal Engineers, Officer of the Legion of Honour, BSc, FIC, PhC, Deputy Controller Chemical Warfare Department, Allies Gas Expert. Lt-Col. Harrison of 57 Chancery Lane and 'Langholm', Sanderstead, died on Monday from heart failure following influenza... Col. Harrison's name will ever be associated with the protection of the British and Allied troops against gas. It is due mainly to his brilliant efforts that throughout the war our troops have been so well protected and that no new gas has ever been employed against us for which his foresight had not completely provided the antidote... He had been responsible for the manufacture of millions of respirators issued to

British, American and Italian troops. Col. Harrison's eldest son had been killed on the Somme on 30th July 1916. Col. Harrison joined up in May 1915 aged 47. (November 1918)

HOLLOWAY, Sapper T., whose home is at Kensington Terrace, Sanderstead, has been awarded the Military Medal, for conspicuous bravery. He was one of the original members of the Sanderstead Fire Brigade and joined the Royal Engineers with other members soon after the outbreak of the war. He is the second member of the brigade who has been rewarded for distinguished services with the British Expeditionary Forces. (January 1917)

JACKSON, Lieutenant George Dewar – Grenadier Guards, was the only son of Mr. & Mrs. Jackson of Sanderstead. He was given a commission in the Grenadier Guards and went to the front in 1915, aged 18. He took part in the Battle of the Somme and was wounded and reported missing in an attack on 15th September 1916. He is now officially presumed to have been killed on that date. He was a very promising young officer and was popular with all ranks. (September 1917)

McGUIRE, Reginald was killed in action on 12th April. He had been a regular member of the Sanderstead Cricket Club 1910-14 and in one first eleven match he created a sensation by starting the bowling and taking five wickets in ten balls. (June 1916)

SMITH, Dr. H. Oswald. The many friends of Dr. Oswald Smith in Croydon and Sanderstead will be pleased that he is returning to his practice after three years of strenuous service in the RAMC of which nearly two years were spent in France. He was badly gassed on 1st April and is only now recovering. Consequent on this he has resigned his commission and returned to Sanderstead. He is receiving a cordial welcome home. (July 1918)

SOURCES

Croydon Advertiser 1914-1919

Coulsdon & Purley Weekly Record 1914-1919

Who's Who

CARPENTER, Capt. A.F.B. (1921). *The Battle of Zeebrugge*

Peace celebrations outside the school – 1919

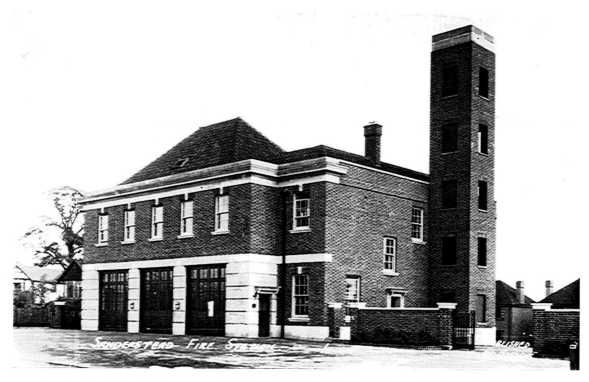

Sanderstead Fire Station, opened 1936, and (below) Phoenix House, built on the site in 1998

Chapter 9

The Old Order Changes – Between the Wars

by Joy Gadsby

Because of financial difficulties, the last hereditary Lord of the Manor, Captain Esme Wigsell Arkwright conveyed the greater part of the Sanderstead estate to Mr. J.G. Hossack in 1919, and the latter sold it in two parts in the same year. Thus began the break-up of the old farming community and the birth of the modern suburb. The development that had begun around the railway stations of Sanderstead and Purley Oaks gathered momentum. Many large houses had already been built before World War I along Sanderstead Road, and other new tree-lined roads – Beech Avenue, East and West Hill, Beechwood Road, Hook Hill and Arkwright Road. Most of the occupants were wealthy enough to keep several servants and all the houses included servants' quarters. A few of these larger houses remain, but most were converted into flats, nursing homes or residential homes for the elderly after World War II, and have subsequently been pulled down to give way to modern blocks of flats.

One of the surviving houses is 'Hurnford House', now divided into flats, but originally belonging to an affluent owner. He employed a gardener for whom he provided a purpose-built cottage which still exists on the corner of Briton Hill Road and Sanderstead Road. With the advent of the motorcar he engaged a chauffeur, and to accommodate him an extension was built onto the gardener's house.

By the late 1920s more modest-sized houses began to appear as the district became much sought-after as a convenient and congenial commuter 'dormitory' for the business classes in the City. The improved rail services and the provision of a bus service along Sanderstead Road from 1921 onwards made it more easily accessible to London. By 1925 development up the hill from the station had reached as far as Briton Hill Road and a resident of that time described how her house was 'literally half in the country and half in the metropolis. To the north there were houses and shops all the way to Westminster; to the south meadows and woods stretched for miles'.

Briton Hill Farmhouse, built in 1883, today stands a little back from the more recent building line, and some of today's elderly residents can still recall chasing cows from the garden and riding on the haycarts that trundled from fields near the present telephone exchange down the unmade track to Briton Hill Farm. Virtually every household had a live-in maid right up until World War II, and every home had a tradesmen's entrance to which the coalman, milkman, baker and greengrocer delivered from horse-drawn carts.

One of the early milk roundsmen was Mr. David Bowerman, who had leased Borough Farm in Limpsfield Road in about 1924. He delivered milk to South Croydon, Purley and Sanderstead and at first the milk was carried by pony and float in a brass-topped 17-gallon churn from which the customers' jugs were filled. Later it was carried in red Trojan vans, and Mr. Bowerman was proud of the fact that the milk was produced and bottled on a local farm. His slogan, painted on the vans, was 'A cow on your doorstep', which from time to time brought comments such as 'we like to keep our doorstep clean, thank you!' The round started at about 4.30 a.m. and finished by about 11 a.m. This meant that in winter the milk was delivered in the dark and there were occasional complaints that 'there was a slug in my milk'. In the days before bottles, some householders put their jugs out overnight to be filled, and the roundsman could not see in the dark if a slug had crept in unawares.

During the 1920s there was little change at the southern end of Sanderstead – the original village – which remained very rural, but in the 1930s private housing began to develop rapidly southwards up the hill. Pressure for land, and better returns from it for residential housing than for agricultural use, gradually saw the break-up of the old farms. Many more roads, with more modest detached or semi-detached houses, quickly filled the gaps, built nevertheless to a fixed minimum standard as befitted what was considered to be a 'select' neighbourhood.

Thus the old estate village at the top of the hill became united – geographically at least – with the northern development. There were however 'two Sandersteads' for many years to come, and residents today still talk about 'going up to the village' and 'down to lower Sanderstead'.

This increased development naturally led to a demand for shops, new or extended churches, sports and leisure facilities, new schools and services of various kinds, and these are more fully described in the following chapters.

Electricity had reached Sanderstead by the 1930s, both for domestic lighting and appliances and for street lighting, although not all minor roads were lit until after World War II.

The telephone exchange was built in 1931 and opened with 814 subscribers.

Telephone Exchange, Church Way, built 1931

A fire station was opened on 26th July 1936, opposite Mitchley Avenue, within easy reach of Hamsey Green. Nevertheless on 13th March 1938 a fire in a garage at Hamsey Green was attended by an engine from Caterham 'as it was in their district'. It took half an hour to arrive! Sanderstead fought hard in the 1990s to keep its fire station but was overruled and it has now been replaced by a block of flats. The library, too, opened in 1936.

Sanderstead continued to be part of Coulsdon and Purley Urban District Council, and was represented at first by four councillors. With the development of Selsdon in 1933, a separate ward was formed for Selsdon and Farleigh, with three councillors, while the representation for Sanderstead was increased to six, each serving for three years. Until World War II both Sanderstead's and Selsdon's councillors stood as Independents, and it was not until 1950 that local elections began seriously to be fought along party political lines, although the first Labour candidates stood in Selsdon as early as 1933 but were heavily defeated.

Fire Brigade 1936
Standing: R H Gould, H Streets
Driver: R Tickner.   3rd Officers: G Ledger & G Tickner
Photograph by Edward B Cook

All this development came to an abrupt halt with the outbreak of World War II in 1939, and from then until the war ended in 1945, Sanderstead citizens, whether from the old village or from the new housing 'down the hill' , united to play their part in the defence of the nation and of their local community.

SOURCES

BOWERMAN, D.   Autobiography - private publication.

Croydon Local Studies Library

HARGREAVES, M. (1977) 'Sanderstead and its Parish Church'   Bourne Society *Local History Records* 16

Minutes of the Sanderstead Ratepayers' Association

Pers. comm. with local residents

PASSING THROUGH a guard of honour of the Auxiliary Territorial Service; Gunner Lester Richards and Volunteer Joan Hewett-Hicks leaving Sanderstead Church after their marriage on Monday.

A newspaper cutting of a wartime wedding, September 1939

Chapter 10

World War II – 1939-1945

by Joy Gadsby

Within minutes of the Prime Minister's speech at 11 o'clock on Sunday, 3rd September 1939, announcing that the country was at war, the air raid sirens sounded over Sanderstead. It was a false alarm, but was a foretaste of what was to become a frequent occurrence during the first two years of the war. Situated as Sanderstead was between the three fighter airfields of Croydon, Kenley and Biggin Hill the residents witnessed many a 'dog fight' overhead as German planes heading for London were intercepted by Hurricanes and Spitfires. There was a contingent of the Polish Airforce stationed at Croydon and so keen were they to get back at the enemy that they took off at lightning speed, just skimming the rooftops, often with their wheels still down. How they missed colliding with the chimney pots was nothing short of a miracle.

The capital was also protected by a ring of barrage balloons and positioned towards Farleigh there was a group of three affectionately christened Faith, Hope & Charity. The local woodlands became a training ground first of all for the Royal Tank Regiment, to be followed by the Irish Guards—the latter billeted in some of the large houses along Sanderstead Road and Sanderstead Hill. Later the Home Guard trained there and the same woods also concealed antiaircraft guns and searchlight crews.

Everyone was involved in one way or another in fighting the war. Younger men and women were conscripted into the armed forces or – in the case of women – into the Land Army or to munitions factories. Older men, and those awaiting call-up joined the Home Guard, to become humorously known as Dad's Army. Others became Air Raid Wardens, members of the Auxiliary Fire Service, the Police War Reserve and other Civil Defence Units. There were ARP posts in strategic places, manned night and day by volunteers, the larger public buildings such as the library, church halls and the telephone exchange being used for the purpose. Air Raid sirens were erected at regular intervals around the village – their wailing warning, occasionally heard even today, still strikes a chill into the hearts of those who grew up with the sound, just as the steady note of the All Clear still brings a sigh of relief.

Public air raid shelters were built in all available suitable places, for example for the school and on the recreation ground, and many householders had their own shelters built in the garden, or strengthened part of their houses – under the stairs being a favourite place to build one. Another precaution taken was the strengthening of windows with a criss-cross pattern of adhesive tape to counteract shattering of the glass from bomb vibrations. Iron railings were donated for the war effort, as were aluminium pots and pans.

Gas masks were supposed to be carried at all times. The civilian ones were less cumbersome than the military version, but were nevertheless very uncomfortable to wear. The face mask was made of black rubber, with a plastic eye-shield, and the mouthpiece consisted of a metal canister containing a charcoal filter. In theory one could breathe freely when wearing a mask, but in practice most people found it extremely difficult. Fortunately they never had to be worn 'for real', but in schools and workplaces drills were frequently held, as of course were fire-drills and evacuation procedures. The gas mask fitted into a small square cardboard box, with a string attached allowing it to be carried round the neck or over the shoulder – a familiar sight, especially where schoolchildren were concerned.

Children too did their bit – collecting tinfoil, waste paper and other scraps of salvage; gathering rose hips in the autumn which were then packed into cardboard boxes and sent free of charge from Sanderstead Station to be turned into rose hip syrup – an essential source of Vitamin C, replacing orange juice, which was seldom obtainable. Others who could knit contributed to the parcels of 'comforts' sent to the troops by the Red Cross; gloves, mittens, scarves, mufflers, pullovers and 'balaclava' helmets, in khaki, navy or air force blue. The quality of the garments was very much dependent on the expertise or otherwise of the knitter!

59th Surrey Batt. Home Guard, " E " Coy.

19 Platoon

DINNER

Sanctuary Restaurant, Selsdon

Saturday, 2nd December, 1944

MENU

BELTING SOUP (a Billing Speciality)
SELSDON PARK HORS D'ŒUVRES

▼

OXTED BEEF   TILLING DOWN LAMB
(Minus Bull's Eyes)
KINGSWOOD PIE

HAMSEY GREENS   H.Q. POTATOES (Well Browned-Off)
SERGT.-MAJOR PEAS (and Q.s Off the Green)

▼

QUEENHILL TART
BIRD SANCTUARY CUSTARD
TITSEY TRIFLE

▼

BISLEY CHEESE
STAND-DOWN COFFEE (Keevils' Special)

▼

BEER FROM THE WOOD
(Gee—Bear and Frith)

Home Guard Dinner – 1944

WORLD WAR II – 1939-1945

Food was rationed but was always adequate. Dried egg powder replaced the real thing and 'Spam' made its debut, being turned into fritters when other meat was short. Some foods disappeared altogether until the end of the war. Many children had no idea what a banana looked like until the war was over. There was a special allocation of food coupons for local organisations – churches, social clubs etc. – to enable life to go on as normally as possible and to keep up the community spirit.

Of course all windows had to be 'blacked out' – hung with thick black curtains so as to exclude any chink of light shining through into the street outside. There were no street lights, and scarcely any traffic to obscure the brightness of the stars. On moonless nights the skies seemed to be full of stars, but cycling home in the dark could be very disorientating. An amusing incident has been recalled by an elderly resident formerly in the Home Guard. On one occasion when on duty at the telephone exchange a very angry wife 'phoned through to report that they were showing a bright light through faulty black-out. It turned out to be the moon reflecting on the windows.

There were two posters frequently displayed. One proclaimed 'Dig for Victory' and gardens and allotments probably had never before – and probably never since – produced so many vegetables and other produce. The other exclaimed 'Careless talk costs lives' – a reminder that enemy spies could be lurking anywhere, tapping phone lines, and overhearing conversations on buses and trains, etc.

There were no signposts – all were removed in anticipation of an invasion, for which there was a real threat in the early days of the war. Station names were obscured, and where possible conspicuous buildings had their roofs camouflaged.

Another wartime innovation was the pig-bin, placed at every street corner for the collection of scraps. These were to remain until well after the war, into the 1950s and were only removed when local residents began to complain about the smell.

At the beginning of the war quite a few local children were evacuated, despite Sanderstead being considered a 'low risk' area. Some went to other remoter parts of the country well away from the capital, and some joined those who went under a special scheme to Canada and the United States for the duration of the war. Sadly not all the ships that sailed across the Atlantic reached their destination. One such was the *City of Benares* which was torpedoed and sunk by a U-boat on 17th September, 1940.

Altogether several hundred bombs fell on Sanderstead – the majority being incendiaries though some heavier high explosive ones were dropped by retreating enemy aircraft jettisoning their loads. On the night of 15th April 1941 there was a particularly heavy incendiary raid over Sanderstead Hill, during which several bombs fell on the roof of All Saints' Church. Thanks to the promptness of the Rector and local firewatchers the fire was very quickly tackled but not without doing considerable damage to the rafters. Services continued however throughout all the weeks that followed, despite the lines of buckets along the nave collecting the rainwater that fell through the holes in the roof.

During the war all church bells were silent, since to ring them was to warn of an invasion – a 20th century equivalent of the Armada beacons!

There was a secret code for calling out the Home Guard in an emergency – the passwords 'Gadfly swat gadfly' passed over the telephone wires were meant to conceal the muster! An elderly resident described an exercise in which the Sanderstead contingent, wearing forage caps, was to wend its way across the fields and capture Whyteleafe Station. It went extremely smoothly. The 'enemy', acted out by Kenley Home Guard wearing berets, was to stop the takeover. The station was duly captured, the Station Master's signature obtained, and his day's takings of 3s. 4½d temporarily confiscated. The 'enemy' was nowhere to be seen. The post-mortem revealed that somehow the administrative wires had been crossed, so that both sides were wearing the same headgear!

Towards the end of the war – in 1944 – after two years of relative freedom from bombing, the first pilotless missiles arrived. V1 flying bombs, given the nickname of 'Doodlebugs' were the first type. They were pilotless midwing monoplanes, propelled by a jet engine. It was an unnerving experience to hear the uneven drone of the engine suddenly cut out, to be followed several seconds later by an explosion. Sadly there were some fatalities and considerable damage in Sanderstead from these infernal machines. Then in the closing months of the war, Hitler launched his V2 rockets – far superior technically and silent in approach. The exploding rocket fell without warning. One such landed in Purley Oaks Road causing a crater eight feet across and almost as deep, and the force of the explosion killed the wife of a gardener as she crossed the open grounds of a nearby house. Her husband, who was indoors, suffered injuries from which he later died.

When Germany surrendered in May 1945 there was spontaneous rejoicing. Street parties were held, bonfires were lit and all the lights were switched on. The church bells rang out for the first time in five years. However, austerity quickly returned as the war in the Far East continued until the surrender of Japan later in the year.

In the years following the war rationing both of food and clothing continued for a time but eventually life became more normal, though very different in atmosphere and tempo from the years before 1939. People looked back nostalgically to the wartime years which were characterised by a shared purpose, comradeship, good humour and resourcefulness. The war was not without its cost – the names of a further 72 men and women were inscribed on Sanderstead's War Memorial, together with those of 13 civilians who lost their lives in the conflict.

East Window of All Saints' Church, Sanderstead, using surviving glass after bomb damage

SOURCES

Croydon Advertiser

Personal and other residents' recollections.

Chapter 11

The Last Fifty Years

by Joy Gadsby

The 50 years since the end of World War II have seen 'progress' at an almost breathtaking pace. Who would have thought in 1945 that by the end of the 20th century almost every household would possess at least one motorcar, freezer and a washing machine; that many would possess a computer, mobile 'phone, dishwasher and video camera; that people would be shopping in supermarkets, buying meals from 'take-aways' and that bank cards of various types would largely have eliminated the need for cash payment. Nor would they have anticipated that many diseases once fatal would now be curable, that transplant surgery could greatly extend life-expectancy, or that television, audio and video recorders would have brought music and popular entertainment into every drawing room at the press of a button. What would they have thought of the Internet, fast foods, double glazing, central heating and the multiplicity of shopping by mail-order?

These advances have not been without their pressures and conflict. The Green Belt, initiated between the wars to stop urban sprawl and provide 'green lungs' for city dwellers, has been under threat from the need for new housing, and an accelerated rise in population. The spread of car ownership has led to a rapid increase in road traffic, with its attendant congestion, pollution, parking restrictions, traffic calming measures and road 'improvements' of one sort or another. With these pressures has come an awakening to the need to conserve our open spaces and an increased interest in our environment and local history.

The roundabout at the top of Sanderstead Hill, constructed in the 1970s to ease traffic congestion

Rectory Court, built on the site of the old rectory, post-1945

On the housing front, estates begun pre-war have been extended and completed. New estates, including social housing, have sprung up, and many of the large old Victorian and Edwardian houses, St. Anne's Convent and the fire station have been pulled down and replaced by modern houses or blocks of flats.

There have been losses as well as gains. Sanderstead has lost to housing many of the fields that still remained immediately after the war and that are remembered with nostalgia. Nevertheless the open spaces still amount to over 50% of the total acreage.

There have been changes, too, in local government. From the 1960s, when the Urban District Council of Coulsdon & Purley was abolished, Sanderstead became part of the London Borough of Croydon – something that was resisted at first but has now come to be accepted by most residents.

On the medical front it is interesting to note that whilst immediately after the war Sanderstead was well served by resident doctors, now most such services again lie outside the parish, as they did in the 19th century!

Where law and order are concerned, crime certainly appears to have increased (though doubtless there was plenty of it in earlier times) but with the development of Neighbourhood Watch schemes attempts are being made to reduce it, with co-operation between the police and the residents.

Social deprivation is not obvious in Sanderstead today, but beneath the veneer of affluence there are many who are lonely and under stress, especially among the increasingly elderly proportion of the population. Against this there has been an upsurge of community care, by organisations such as Rotary, Neighbourhood Care and

Churches Together. The Residents' Association is well supported and keeps a watchful eye on planning applications and developments that might affect the quality of life, as does also the Bourne Society, and there is more co-operation today between the different sections of the community, north and south of the 'village'.

Some institutions have been lost ; banks and some local shops have been forced to close or relocate while others struggle to survive. Boundary changes – extending the Croydon municipal boundary to the centre of Tithepit Shaw Lane, have procured Sanderstead a pub – *The Good Companions* – for the first time in its history and bus passes for elderly folk who were missing out at the southern end of Hamsey Green.

Developments in education, public transport and church building have been well documented elsewhere in this book.

For all these changes, most would say that Sanderstead, though no longer a 'village' in the traditional sense is still a good place to live, and will remain so as residents increasingly take responsibility for its welfare, participate in its social and corporate life and play their part in cherishing their history, and conserving what is best in their inheritance.

Cedar Court, built in the 1970s, viewed from the church roof

Sanderstead Village School 1831

Chapter 12

Education Then and Now

By Francis Davison

The National School

Elementary education came comparatively early to Sanderstead, at least by English standards. Before the Education Act of 1870, responsibility for providing elementary education rested, not with local or national government, but with the churches. The 'National Society for the Education of the Poor according to the Principles of the Church of England' represented the Anglican interest and the 'British and Foreign School Society' that of the Nonconformists. Both bitterly opposed the intervention of the state in education, though they accepted some very limited funding from the Exchequer. In Sanderstead a 'National School' seems to have been founded by 1831. A drawing dated 1831 is labelled 'The Village School' and shows a large house. There is no record of its establishment but the census of 1841 mentions a teacher and a 'home of a teacher' and the Tithe Apportionment Map of 1843 shows the school in a cottage opposite 'The White House'. In 1873 an inquiry was held into the provision of education in each parish. The return for Sanderstead showed that the National School was housed in a single school room which was owned by Col.Wigsell. The School was managed by Col. Wigsell and the Rector. The teacher was Helena Hawes, there were 25 boys and 33 girls on the roll, and the fees were 1d a week. The total of 58 pupils compares well with the average attendances of 40 to 47 at the Board School, reported in the 1880s. The school probably taught virtually all the village's children, though we do not know the quality of the teaching. The single schoolmistress was probably unqualified. The school would have been inspected, at least in theory, by inspectors approved by the National Society, as well as by Col. Wigsell and the Rector.

The Board School (Now Gresham School)

In 1875 Sanderstead established a School Board of five members, with S.J. Cowdrey as its clerk. Col. Wigsell donated land and the school, designed to hold 75 pupils, was built at a cost of £1,310. The original building is part of Gresham School today. The new school opened in 1876. The first head teacher was probably Miss Anne Kezia Hause. She was certainly in charge in 1878. The new school building was never filled at this time. Local directories reported average attendances as follows:

1882	40
1887	47
1890	65
1895	64
1899	54

Sanderstead was unusual in allowing a National School to be replaced by a nondenominational Board School. A much more common practice, followed for instance at Purley and Addington, was to keep a Church School in being but to take advantage of the public funding newly available. The Church would in such cases retain the responsibility for providing the premises, while the ratepayers met the running costs. In the case of a Board School all costs were met from the rates, except for the very small proportion still met by school fees. Only the very poor received free education. In 1891 fees for elementary education were abolished. Attendance at school was compulsory between the ages of five and 13, but there is evidence that a number of children left early to take up employment, while absences were common at harvest time.

Surrey County Council Takes Over Education

In 1889 the Technical Instruction Act gave County Councils responsibility for 'technical and manual instruction' and they began to provide a very limited number of scholarships for pupils at elementary schools to study for three years at grammar schools. Initially there were 36 scholarships for the whole County, so the likelihood of anyone from Sanderstead winning one was not great. For a boy who was successful there could have been a place at Whitgift Middle School.

Census returns for 1871 and 1881 show a small number of apprentices in various trades living in Sanderstead. Apprenticeships continued into the present century, and some apprentices were expected to gain theoretical knowledge to support their practical skills by attending evening classes. There is no record of such classes in Sanderstead, and apprentices would have had to travel perhaps to the County Council's Technical Institute, housed in a prefabricated iron hut in the grounds of Purley National School, and opened in about 1890.

The 1902 Education Act transferred responsibility for elementary education to the County Council and Sanderstead's Board School became the Council School. The County Council did a lot to expand educational provision in other parts of the county, but little changed in Sanderstead. The village school was adequate for the old village on the hilltop, but was very inconvenient and inaccessible to the growing population living in the new houses near the stations in the north of the parish. For many the South Croydon Primary School (now Purley Oaks School) would have been very convenient. However, that school was for the citizens of Croydon and the County Council refused to pay for Sanderstead pupils to attend there. Instead pupils had the choice of walking up the hill to the village school (as there was no bus service until 1921) or going to Purley Church of England School (now Christ Church School, then located in Purley High Street) or Roke Primary School on the borders of Kenley.

Sanderstead Village School, built 1875, photographed in 1907

Mrs Small (sitting), Head of the Village School, Mrs Cowdrey and 'Gyp'.

c. 1916

Grammar school provision did creep a little nearer as the century progressed. Purley Boys' Grammar School was founded in 1914 in Godstone Road. When it moved to Placehouse Lane, Old Coulsdon, in 1933, Purley Girls' Grammar School was established in the vacated building. Before that Whyteleafe Girls' County Secondary School, founded in 1907 offered a grammar school education for girls. Most grammar school pupils at this time had to pay fees, though there were some scholarships available.

Selsdon Primary and Central Schools

During the late 1920s the population of Selsdon grew dramatically as the Costain estate was built, and the new inhabitants included a high proportion of young middle class couples with children. The County Council's response was to build Selsdon Primary School, which opened in 1928 and which was the first school in Selsdon. It was followed by Selsdon Central School, opened in 1931. Both occupied the same building in Addington Road. The new schools were immediately popular, so much so that in 1931 the old Sanderstead village school had to close for lack of pupils.

Response to the Growth of Population in the 1930s

The growth of population in Sanderstead soon reversed this closure. The village school reopened in 1933 with 11 pupils. By 1935 there were 78 pupils, and the village hall by the recreation ground had to be used as an overflow classroom. In December 1936 work was started on a new building behind the old one, and by November 1937 three new classrooms were available for use. Work on the extension was completed in 1938 and the old building was converted into a dining room.

Upper School, Sanderstead, 1920

Despite these developments, demand for educational facilities continued to expand faster than supply, and there was a strong feeling in the area that Sanderstead and Selsdon – tucked away in one of the extremities of the County – were being neglected by Surrey County Council. During the 1930s the local Residents' Associations complained and campaigned. In 1936 a survey showed the following pattern of secondary education for Sanderstead and Selsdon pupils—

School	Capacity	Sanderstead Total	Sanderstead Scholarship	Selsdon Total	Selsdon Scholarship
Purley Boys'	490	19	3	36	9
Purley Girls'	240	12	4	8	5
Whyteleafe Girls'	240	20	6	17	11
St. Anne's R.C.	?	?	7	?	3
Total		51 +	20	61 +	28

In addition to these schools many of the pupils at the four Croydon independent grammar schools came from Surrey, 50% at Croydon High, 25% at Whitgift, 21% at Old Palace and 10 % at Whitgift Middle School (now Trinity). Many of these were from Sanderstead and Selsdon. To attend any grammar school meant paying fees unless you had a scholarship. The annual fees at the time were:

Croydon High School	£8 10s. 0d
Maintained Grammar Schools	£12 0s. 0d
Old Palace School	£16 0s. 0d
Whitgift Middle School	£15 0s. 0d
Whitgift School	£30 0s. 0d

These arrangements were not considered satisfactory by many of those living in the area. A conference was organised in 1937, involving the Ratepayers' Association of Sanderstead and the Residents' Associations of Hamsey Green, Selsdon and Riddlesdown, to consider the provision of a new secondary school in the area. The conference was unanimous in urging the County Council to go ahead with the building of a new secondary school for boys and girls upon the land in Mitchley Wood, which the County Council had already acquired. They also pressed for the building of a new primary school in Tithepit Shaw Lane, the provision of transport for children in the Riddlesdown area to local schools, and the making available of Croydon Schools to those living in the north of the parish. None of these requests had been met by the time war broke out in 1939.

Not all the local citizens agreed with the campaign. One resident wrote to the Sanderstead Ratepayers' Association, in 1937, that 'there are plenty of excellent private schools in the locality and the Whitgift is only a mile away. If any ratepayer wants public charity in the shape of a Board School education for his children I suggest he moves to a locality where such schools exist. I, for one, don't want a Board School planted in Sanderstead.' This was clearly a minority view, however.

The Effects of War on the Schools

World War I does not seem to have had much direct impact on the village school. Although there were air raids on London by Zeppelins and Gothas, these did not affect Sanderstead. However, in 1918 the School Managers made representations to the officer in charge of the local aerodrome, calling attention to the 'reckless manner in which machine gun practice is carried on in the vicinity of the school' and asked that they should stop using the target at Miller's Farm. The end of the war was marked by a celebration at the school, recorded in a photograph, which shows how pleased the pupils were that peace had come. (See page 57)

World War II had much more impact and the danger from the air was much greater. On 4th September all the local schools were closed until air raid shelters were available. By 28th September trenches had been dug at the village school, and the children attended to practise air raid drill and to have their gas masks inspected and fitted. Normal school was resumed on 2nd October, but numbers were limited by the capacity of the trenches. Infants attended only half time, and school hours were adjusted to allow children to be home before dark and 'to allow at least an hour for cleaning before blackout time'.

By March 1940 work had begun to turn the lower corridor into an air raid shelter. On 12th and 25th September bombs fell in the Recreation Ground and in the field behind the school but did not explode and the school was closed until they were exploded on 12th October. Air raids continued to affect attendance and in 1944 the flying bombs did much damage to the area but none fell on or near the village school. 8th and 9th May 1945 were marked by the closure of the school to celebrate VE Day.

Life in an Elementary School

The curriculum in elementary schools was simple and basic. There was a concentration on the 'three R's'. In the village school cookery and gardening classes were introduced in 1909. The Head Teacher's garden was used for the gardening classes and the caretaker, who seems also to have been the Head Teacher's husband, was appointed gardening instructor.

In the 1920s the pupils at the village school from the local cottages and farms were very poor. They had to walk to school, often over long distances, and had to bring their own – generally frugal – lunches. The Head Teacher, Mrs Small, provided them with milk or hot soup to supplement these.

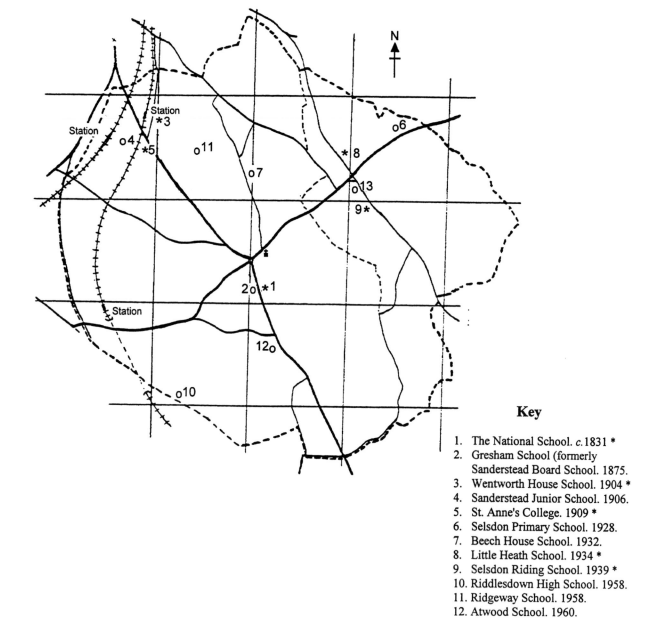

Key

1. The National School. *c.*1831 *
2. Gresham School (formerly Sanderstead Board School. 1875.
3. Wentworth House School. 1904 *
4. Sanderstead Junior School. 1906.
5. St. Anne's College. 1909 *
6. Selsdon Primary School. 1928.
7. Beech House School. 1932.
8. Little Heath School. 1934 *
9. Selsdon Riding School. 1939 *
10. Riddlesdown High School. 1958.
11. Ridgeway School. 1958.
12. Atwood School. 1960.
13. Croydon High School. 1966.

o Denotes an existing school.
* Denotes a school now closed.

DEVELOPMENT OF SCHOOLS IN SANDERSTEAD AND SELSDON

A report on the school by one of His Majesty's Inspectors – in 1938 – said that 'the children on the whole are good material and the Headmistress has the active co-operation of interested parents. Thus, in spite of the difficulties that, of necessity, attend a school in a growing district, the school is in most respects doing well. Written English is very good in the two top classes. Arithmetic is, at the moment, less successful, but the teaching is systematic and competent and progress can be expected. Drawing is good and handiwork gives promise of developing well. The singing was clear and lively'.

One local resident, Joyce Eeles, has recorded her memories of the school—

'In 1933 I was sent to the village school in Limpsfield Road, now called Gresham School. This had been closed since 1930 through lack of pupils, but with the new building spree it managed to find eight boys and girls. The red-brick building is the same from the outside today. Inside then, there was a narrow area by the front door, used as a cloakroom. The two rooms were the classrooms. Open fires heated the place, and if you wanted to stay for lunch, you brought your own. In front of the school, bordering the Limpsfield Road, was an enormous round flower bed. Each pupil had a slice of this to look after and weeding it was counted as the nature study lesson. Education was directed from Kingston, and the only sign of official interest seemed to be from a retired army colonel who dropped in unannounced from time to time. Everyone stood to attention and said nothing except their name. His sole interest was in the school register, which he went through to make sure the teacher had filled it in correctly!'

Post War Developments

The 1944 Education Act provided secondary education for all children, but it took some time before the new facilities were available in Sanderstead. The campaign by local organisations to demand better educational facilities, which had been suspended during the war, was resumed. An Education Campaign Council was formed in 1946, supported by the Residents' Associations of Sanderstead, Selsdon and Riddlesdown, the Sanderstead Women's Institute, the Sanderstead Housing League, the Sanderstead and Selsdon Communist Party, the Sanderstead Liberal Party, and the Labour and Conservative Parties of Sanderstead and Selsdon. Their objectives were very similar to those of the pre-war campaign—a secondary school at Riddlesdown; a new primary school at Hamsey Green; transport for children – especially the very young – who had a long walk to school, and temporary classrooms at existing schools as a stopgap. The Education Campaign Council continued to operate until 1955, although the political parties had withdrawn their membership at an earlier date to enable the campaign to be non-political.

The campaign bore some fruit. In 1949 a primary school was opened in Tithepit Shaw Lane in Hamsey Green, and in January 1958 Riddlesdown School was opened as a mixed secondary modern school, on a site that had been purchased in the 1930s. In 1969 Riddlesdown School was converted to a comprehensive school, catering for students aged 11 to 16, and in 1996 it introduced a sixth form, taking the age range up to 18.

The 1950s and 1960s were a time of growth. Ridgeway School was opened in February 1958 as a combined Infants' and Junior School. In 1963 the infants' department was hived off as a separate infants' school, though in the same building. Atwood County Primary School opened in June 1960.

During the 1950s adult education became available in the parish for the first time, when an Adult Education Centre was established by the County Council, while the Sanderstead and Selsdon Branch of the Workers' Education Association held its first meeting at the village school on 18th March 1952. The first chairman was Mr R.A.Doffett and the branch had 15 members.

Transfer to Croydon

On 1st April 1965, Sanderstead, along with the rest of the Coulsdon and Purley Urban District, became part of the London Borough of Croydon, which took over all Surrey County Council's responsibilities in the area, including education. One immediate effect was to open to Sanderstead students the conveniently accessible educational facilities of Croydon. The newly available resources ranged from Purley Oaks Primary School to

Croydon's College of Art and Technical College. Today substantial numbers of students from the north of the borough travel daily to Riddlesdown School, while Sanderstead students have a wide choice of secondary schools to choose from, as well as Croydon College and the John Ruskin and Purley Sixth Form colleges.

Private Schools in Sanderstead

In parallel with the growth of publicly-financed education, Sanderstead has been the home of many independent schools. Many of these have been small and fairly short-lived, but several have had a long and successful life. The setting up of private schools came in two waves. The first, in the north of the parish, ran from 1903 to 1916. The second occurred during the 1930s and covered Selsdon and the southern part of Sanderstead, catering for the inhabitants of the new estates being built at that time.

During the first phase at least seven private schools were established. Of these, one is still running; one ran for 71 years, one for 28 years, and two more for over a decade.

The second period of rapid growth, between 1930 and 1939 saw the establishment of at least 11 private schools, but of these only one survives to this day. The bulk of the others appear to have been killed off by the war.

— Sanderstead Junior School

Sanderstead Junior School was founded by Mrs Harrison on 6th January 1906, and has continued to teach pupils ever since. It has a longer continuous history in the parish than any other school. The school is located at 29 Purley Oaks Road. The original building was of corrugated iron and the interior was of dark brown wood. It consisted of one moderately-sized room and two tiny rooms, together with a small toilet with a yellow 'kitchen sink'. The present building is much larger and better equipped and would be unrecognisable to the original pupils. The school still admits boys and girls aged from 3 to 12.

— St Anne's College

In the early years of this century the only Roman Catholic girls' school in the area was Coloma, and there was nothing available for Catholics living in South Croydon, Sanderstead or Purley. To remedy this a secondary school was established in Sanderstead Road, just east of the railway. When it started, on 12th September 1909, it had two classrooms and 12 children, and the building was not yet complete. The establishment of a Roman Catholic School aroused opposition from some Protestants. Groups preached outside the school against 'Papists invading this part of the country' and stones were thrown through windows, so that no lights could be shown to the front. Despite this opposition the College grew and flourished, expanding physically with the building of extensions and new wings and the purchase of the house next door.

St Anne's College
pre-war

In l939, with the outbreak of war, 90 of the girls were evacuated to 'Hatchlands', East Clandon. The college in Sanderstead had to be closed until an air raid shelter had been built. The school then reopened, but with only four nuns remaining to carry out teaching 250 pupils.

In 1944 flying bombs brought new danger, and the whole school was evacuated to Dunblane in Scotland until the end of the war in 1945.

The years after the war were marked by continuing success and expansion. In the mid-1970s the sixth-formers from John Fisher School came to share lessons in A-Level Classics and Ancient History. One of the boys commented that 'Three times a week we leave the noisy corridors littered with cricket bats, rugger balls and small boys, for the freshly painted, antiseptic cloisters of St Anne's, where teachers call you by your Christian name and smile while they are telling you off. When girls pass you in the corridors they either scream or burst out laughing, and once a week they all go to Forum and talk about jumping out of balloons.'

Despite its success the College was eventually found to be too small and in 1990 it was amalgamated with Coloma R.C. Girls' School and the site sold and redeveloped, but the wall and railings in Sanderstead Road have been left intact and on the gates you can still see the insignia of the Ladies of Mary. A Bourne Society plaque to commemorate the school can also be seen there.

— Wentworth House School

The third of the long-lasting schools founded in the first period of development was Wentworth House School, at 28 Mayfield Road. It was founded in 1904 by Miss E.A.Morgan LL.A. and Miss E.Robinson ACP. It catered for boys and girls up to the age of 11 and had about 20 pupils. These two ladies continued to run it until about 1934 and continued to live at the house thereafter, having presumably retired.

— Beech House School

Beech House School was founded in 1932 by Miss Whistler and Miss Christopherson. It catered for boys and girls aged four to eleven and was located, then as now, at 15 Church Way. Miss Whistler and Miss Christopherson were succeeded after a few years by Miss Head, who was described as 'very kind and loving but very strict'. In the 1930s the school had about 25 pupils. Today it has about 40 pupils aged between three and seven.

— Little Heath School

Little Heath School at 66 Farley Road, Selsdon, opened in 1927 by Miss M.Stainton LRAM. It managed to survive World War II, teaching pupils of nursery and infant age groups. It closed about 1964. The last Headmistress was Mrs Aphele. (Photograph overleaf)

Croydon High School for Girls

With the expansion of the quantity and quality of state educational facilities, the scope for small private schools has declined and since the war there has been no crop of new private schools in Sanderstead. In 1966, however, Croydon's oldest girls' independent school moved to Selsdon. Croydon High School for Girls was founded in 1874, at a site in North End, by the Girls' Public Day School Trust. It was the third school founded by the Trust, and from its foundation has had a very high academic reputation. In 1880 it moved to Wellesley Road, and by 1966 it had outgrown this site and moved to new premises in Old Farleigh Road, Selsdon. There it has maintained its excellent reputation, drawing students from a wide area around Croydon. However its arrival in its new site marked a significant enhancement of the local educational facilities.

Selsdon Park Riding School

Selsdon Park Riding School was not, of course, a school in the same sense as the others described above, but it was one of the educational opportunities, though not academic, that was available to local people. It was established in Old Farleigh Road in about 1939 and was still operating there in 1959, but has since moved to Farleigh.

A HISTORY OF SANDERSTEAD

SOURCES

Atwood School Prospectus

Census returns for 1841, 1851, 1861, 1871 and 1881

COX. R.C.W., Croydon School Archives

EELES, JOYCE (1982) 'Sanderstead in the 1920s' Bourne Society *Local History Records* 21

GADSBY, JOY. (1990) 'Continuity and Change in Sanderstead, from Rural Village to Commuter Suburb: the Role of Education'

Gresham Primary School, 1875-1975, Sanderstead. Centenary Booklet.

HIGHAM, A., (Ed.) (1996) *Village Histories. 1. Purley.*, Bourne Society

KEENAN. S.E. *St Anne's College - One School's Life*

Minutes of Sanderstead Residents' Association

Minutes of Selsdon Residents' Association

ROBINSON. D. *Surrey Through the Century 1889-1989*

Sanderstead Tithe Map of 1843

Surrey Trade Directories

Ward's Directories of Croydon and Purley

Pers. comm. from Alison Barnes, Brian Stocker, Ellen Rosier and the principal of Beech House School.

Little Heath School 1929

Tony Jordan Dennis Walter Joan Wilder Dorothy Hodson Peggy Walter Ann Barker Marjorie Harrison
Kathleen Starr   ?   Diana Baker Alan Smith ?Phyllis Church Joan Herbert   ?   Ralph Law
Robert Huggett Valerie Cherry ?Tony Mumford Eileen Clutterbuck Michael Coleman Evelyn Langdon John Howard
?   ?   ?John Grant Ronnie Parrot ?Marie Turner   ?   ? Margaret Gulland

(Photo courtesy of Kathleen Starr)

Chapter 13

Communications – Moving onto the Fast Track

by Terry Carroll

Trackways and Roads

With the exception of the Roman roads, and roads which were designed and built from the late 17th century, the ages of most of the roads and trackways now visible are unknown and will probably remain so.

On the western boundary of Sanderstead there is evidence of a Roman road across Riddlesdown. Part of the road from London to Lewes, through Croydon and Caterham, was diverted onto the slopes of Riddlesdown to avoid the marshy and sometimes flooded banks of the Bourne in the valley bottom. The slope was terraced to provide a level platform for the road and this terracing can still be seen.

The earliest inhabitants of whom there is evidence were Mesolithic hunter/gatherers *c.*10,000 BC to 4000 BC who would have followed their prey along well-worn animal tracks. There is also evidence that they and their successors settled on the higher ground and so probably the earliest well-defined trackways were on the line of the present Limpsfield Road. This crosses the plateau of the North Downs southwards towards Titsey Hill and northwards towards Selsdon where it joined a pre-Roman trackway from the Sussex iron deposits to the Thames valley via Croham Hurst and Croydon. Archaeological finds dating from Mesolithic times onwards give credence to this conjecture.

From *c.*4000 BC the lifestyle of the people became more settled, and a network of lanes and tracks developed linking farm with farm and village with village. In Domesday Book, the manors of Addington, Croydon, Ham, Coulsdon, Waddington and Sanderstead are recorded and we can be reasonably sure that the settlements they represented were linked by trackways. Croydon subsequently became an important market centre which would have made those trackways leading to it subject to frequent movements of cattle, sheep and materials. Limpsfield Road probably developed in importance in this way.

In the Middle Ages travel was mainly by horseback or on foot with heavy goods being conveyed in oxcarts and on pack-horses. Coaches were first introduced into England *c.*1555. John Ownstead, who was Lord of the Manor soon after that time, was 'Serjeant of Her Majestie's Carriage' to Elizabeth I for 40 years and as such was responsible for providing transport for her many journeys across England.

The first stage coaches carrying goods and passengers began in England *c.*1640, and by the 18th century there was a regular coaching route through Croydon to Brighton using more or less the line of the present A22 but following the old Roman road across Riddlesdown. In 1776 it cost 6s.6d. to travel by coach from London to Lewes and half-price for children. In 1808 it cost 23s. 0d from Brighton to London but only 13s. 0d from London to Brighton.

The increasing wheeled traffic led to measures to maintain and improve the roads, which were getting into a very bad state of repair. Turnpike Trusts were authorised by Parliament for this purpose, the first turnpike road in Surrey being that between Crawley and Reigate, opened in 1696. Although Sanderstead was comparatively remote from the hurly burly of the coaching routes, the road which is now the B269 from South Croydon through Sanderstead to Botley Hill was considered important enough to merit the Limpsfield Road Trust being set up in 1813. It lasted, as did most of the 1000 or more other Trusts, until their winding-up by law during the 1860s and 1870s. The coming of the railways played a major part in their demise although the Limpsfield Trust's income was probably less affected than most.

An example of the charges levied reads: A gig 6d, a horse and cart 4½d, saddle horses 1½d, drove of horses and cows ½d each, sheep ¼d. There were exceptions, such as for soldiers, churchgoers and mail coaches; all traffic had to give way to the latter. Costs of maintenance and interest varied greatly between the Trusts. Those for the Surrey and Sussex Trust were £335 per mile in the 1830s, whilst those for the Limpsfield Trust were £23. Little evidence remains of tollgates and tollhouses on Limpsfield Road. There is a reference to toll-bars at Hamsey Green in 1828 and there is still a toll house standing by the side of the road at Botley Hill. There must have been other toll points along the 12 miles of road under the Trust's care; by 1850 Surrey had an average of one every three miles.

In 1889 the newly-formed County Councils took over responsibility for the maintenance of main roads and in 1894 the Rural District Councils that for the local roads. However, it was not until 1909 that central Government made any grants to local authorities in respect of roads. With the population in the parish changing little from the time of Domesday until the coming of the railway to Sanderstead in 1884, there was little need for roads to carry wheeled traffic heavier than the occasional horse-drawn cart or carriage. An exception was Limpsfield Road, with its traffic of a mainly through nature to and from the markets in Croydon. The usual construction of the main roads was of graded broken stone, watered and rolled to form a hard and fairly even surface. The ample supply of local flints would in this instance have been an economic asset.

Mrs Cowdrey and Mrs Small in the cab from Sanderstead Station   pre-1921

Photographs of Sanderstead Hill and Limpsfield Road indicate that the road surface was still unbound in the early 1920s, but with the increase in the number of heavy motor vehicles it was soon necessary to strengthen the roads and seal them with surfacings made of tar or bitumen macadam or with a layer of concrete. By the beginning of World War II there were few adopted roads left in the parish which had unsealed surfaces.

Although there has been an enormous increase in the built-up area of Sanderstead since the beginning of the century, the pattern of roads forming the main arteries of the parish has remained substantially the same as that shown on Rocque's map of 1764. A major exception is the route along Rectory Park and Mitchley Avenue, from

Sanderstead to Purley, constructed in the early 1930s. There have been many road widenings and traffic schemes over the years but except for the large roundabout at the top of Sanderstead Hill there has been none involving major works.

There have been two transient threats of motorways running through the heart of Sanderstead. The first – in the 1960/70s – was a tentative suggestion appearing on the Greater London Development Plan for Ringway Three to run east to west a ¼ mile or so south of the crossroads at the top of Sanderstead Hill. The idea of having three ring roads around London in addition to the M25 evaporated once their cost had been fully assessed .The second threat arose in the 1980s, when there was a proposal to build a motorway to link a proposed crossing of the River Thames near Woolwich with the M25 near Godstone. One of the alternative routes was aligned to pass near the top of Sanderstead Hill. The storm of protest from a crowded outdoor meeting held in Sanderstead was added to that from other communities along the proposed line. This, coupled with the heavy construction costs involved, soon persuaded the Secretary of State for Transport to abandon the proposal.

Railways

As early as 1841 a railway line had been opened from London to Brighton, passing for nearly 1 km through the parish. The nearest stations were Godstone Road (which later became Caterham Junction and finally Purley) and East Croydon. The section of line passing within the bounds of Sanderstead was owned by the company soon to become part of the London, Brighton and South Coast Railway (LBSCR) whilst the South Eastern Railway (SER) had running powers over the same section of line. The SER opened the first main line service to Dover via Redhill and Tonbridge in 1844. For the next 60 years there were disputes and bickerings – but also some co-operation – between the two companies as they manoeuvred to establish new lines and increase their earning power in the territory to the east of the London to Brighton line. Much has been written elsewhere describing these events, but suffice it to say here that this state of affairs played a major part in governing if and when Sanderstead would eventually have a station of its own.

Without a conveniently placed station, the effect of the railway on the life of the people in Sanderstead would have been limited. However, the more affluent members of the village community would have been able to use the new mode of transport, using their carrriages and horses to travel to and from East Croydon station.

Goods were brought by rail to local stations, and there is an account of a wagon belonging to the owner of 'Sanderstead Court' going down to East Croydon Station to collect tons of coal, the horses 'all caparisoned as if they were going to a show in Hyde Park', reflecting the continuation of customs of many years' standing. This was at the turn of the century, some years after Sanderstead and Purley Oaks had acquired their own stations.

In 1865 the LBSCR – to pre-empt any further expansion by the SER into territory that the LBSCR considered to be its own – made an arrangement with the newly-formed Surrey & Sussex Junction Railway (SSJR) for the latter to obtain powers from Parliament to construct a line from Croydon to Groombridge, thus cutting across territory disputed by the two major companies, with the intention of providing, in due course, access to Tunbridge Wells, Lewes, Brighton and Eastbourne.

Local eminent people who gave evidence to a House of Commons Select Committee included Captain Atwood Wigsell, Lord of the Manor, who owned 3000 acres (most of the parish). He said that he had a provisional agreement with the Company that they would provide him with a station, but there is no record as to its possible location.

The line was authorised by Parliament in July 1865, to run from a junction with the Brighton line close to South Croydon station, its route passing for about 3¼ km. through lower Sanderstead and under part of Riddlesdown. Waring was the contractor. Work including the initial boring of the Riddlesdown tunnel, bridges and the brick viaduct at Woldingham had been advanced when financial backing began to dry up after an important firm of financiers, Overend and Gurney, failed in 1866. As a result ownership of the works was transferred to the LBSCR in 1869, who then sought powers to abandon them. These were refused by Parliament who also imposed a maximum penalty of £32,250 if there were to be failure to complete the line. As the Company had estimated the cost of completion to be as much as £2 million, it chose to pay the penalty and abandon the works, which soon became obscured under shrubs and other vegetation.

The urge to open up the territory to the east of the Brighton line remained irresistible, and in June 1878 after joint discussions and in agreement with the SER, the LBSCR obtained an Act of Parliament 'to complete and construct Railways between Croydon, Oxted and East Grinstead', with the section of the new line between South Croydon and where it crossed the SER's line at Crowhurst (Surrey) to be jointly owned. The completion time allowed by the Act was four years with a non-completion penalty of £50 per day. Joseph Firbank, for whom the company had a high regard, obtained the contracts for the whole line.

Although Waring had made a start ten years earlier, Firbank still had most of the heavy works to carry out beyond Woldingham, as well as the major task of completing what Waring had left unfinished. The extent of the completed works can be gauged from the following list of major items—

> 1,660,000 cubic metres of earthworks; 3340 metres of brick-lined tunnel, including 765 under
> Riddlesdown; 57 bridges, 4 viaducts; 30 kilometres of double track line

Despite some difficulties, especially with the diversion of water from heavy springs encountered in the Oxted tunnel, construction was finished within the stipulated time. The line was officially inspected in February 1884 by Major-General Hutchinson, who reported that 'the lines are altogether well finished and the works of a substantial character'. The line was opened to the public on 10th March 1884, but there was apparently little or no celebration of the occasion. To give the SER an access to Tonbridge from its mid-Kent line at Woodside, a link was built to a junction with the Oxted line at Selsdon Road; the contractor was Joseph Firbank. The link was opened in August 1885, to be jointly operated by SER and LBSCR in alternate years and giving an alternative route to London for Sanderstead passengers.

With the presence of a station in Sanderstead, albeit close to the northern boundary, impetus was given to house-building in the immediate vicinity, and when the LBSCR quadrupled the main Brighton line from South Croydon to Coulsdon in November 1899, a new station was opened at Purley Oaks. However the effect further afield remained small.

Like most other lines, the Oxted line through Sanderstead has not been without some unusual features. One was the halt provided by the LBSCR/SER for the benefit of the golfers of Purley Downs Golf Club for part of the time between 1914 and 1927. It was situated close to the bridge over the railway in Purley Downs Road. Before the motor car became the usual way of travel to golf clubs, the railways provided the best and quickest means of reaching many of them. As a result, they were willing to negotiate discounted fares with the clubs and even to build footbridges and halts for the convenience of club members.

In 1923 the LBSCR and the SER became part of the Southern Railway (SR) which had a co-operative attitude towards builders siting the new housing estates near its lines; subsequently Riddlesdown Station was opened in June 1927. It was built on open downland near the northern portal of Riddlesdown tunnel and marked the end of railway-building in the parish. In June 1986 the main station building on the 'up' platform at Sanderstead was very badly damaged by fire. Arson was not suspected. It was replaced by a new brick building, with a refurbishment of the rest of the station to match.

Whenever electrification proposals for the Oxted line were put forward by the SR, they were invariably deferred. Surprisingly, the line from Woodside to Sanderstead had been electrified in 1935, although it had in fact never proved to be an economic success. Notwithstanding this in 1935 a half-hourly service of electric trains was introduced between Sanderstead and Charing Cross or Cannon Street using the Woodside link. It did not prove to be a success, and when World War II came, the service was drastically cut. These cuts remained after the war, to become ever more drastic until the passenger service was finally withdrawn in 1983. The track from north of Selsdon to Woodside was abandoned soon afterwards.

COMMUNICATIONS – MOVING ONTO THE FAST TRACK

Staff at Purley Oaks Station, early 20th century

The last train on the Woodside –Sanderstead service - 1983

A HISTORY OF SANDERSTEAD

Whilst the electric service faded from Sanderstead Station, the other services on the Oxted line flourished, at first providing the only remaining steam-hauled trains regularly passing through East Croydon Station, which continued until 1962. Modernisation followed owing to the steady increase in the number of commuters, and the first of 19 three-car diesel-electric multiple units (DMUs) went into action, augmented during peak periods by a few diesel locomotive-hauled trains, the coaches being of a 'certain age' with corridors and plush seating. The last steam locomotive reported to have passed through Sanderstead was No: 34108 *Wincanton*, an express West Country-class light Pacific heading an enthusiasts' special in March 1967 — a fitting conclusion to the steam era.

No. 34108 'Wincanton' heading the last regular steam service through Selsdon. March 1967
Photo courtesy of the *Croydon Advertiser*

The future of the Oxted line inevitably came under scrutiny when Dr. Richard Beeching was appointed Chairman of the Transport Commission in 1961, with instructions to review the commercial viability of Britain's railway system. When the 'Beeching cuts' came it was the section of line beyond Uckfield which ceased to operate; the knock-on effect on the Oxted line traffic was small.

In the mid-1980s British Railways (BR) instituted an independent financial appraisal, which indicated that electrification of the line as far as East Grinstead and using second-hand rolling stock would give the best return. In addition there were enough DMUs available to maintain the diesel service from Oxted to Uckfield for the time being. The proposal was authorised in May 1985, the work completed within the estimated cost of nearly £7 million, and the electrified system was operational by the end of September 1987.

The opportunity was also taken to modernise and renovate the entire line. It was at this time that Sanderstead gained its rebuilt station, and an up-to-date signalling system was installed, controlled from a new box at Oxted. Sanderstead Station had until this time provided an unusual feature. The signal box was sited in the middle of

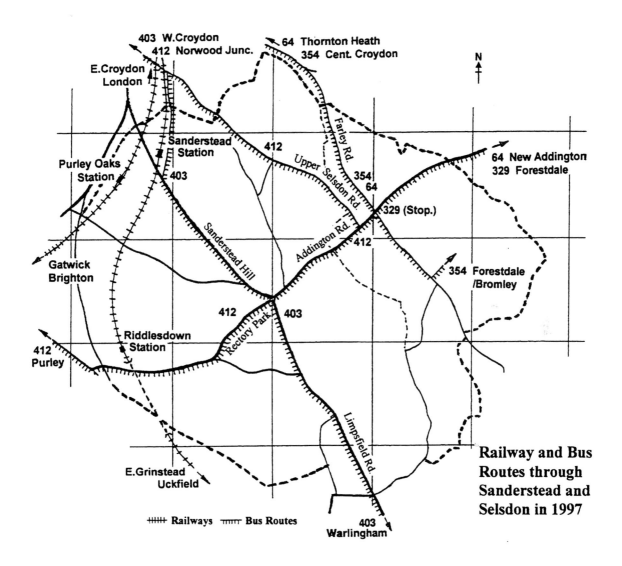

Railway and Bus Routes through Sanderstead and Selsdon in 1997

the 'down' platform. This arrangement had at least two benefits – the signalman was afforded easy and sheltered access to his place of work and passengers were able to get firsthand information as to the up-to-the-minute state of running of the trains.

In contrast to the muted opening of the line over 103 years before, BR was inspired to arrange an 'Electrification Gala' over the weekend of 26th/27th September, with intensive train services and tied-in offers for local attractions near a number of stations along the line to East Grinstead. The Secretary of State for Transport formally opened the service on 30th September 1987, and the full public service commenced on Monday 5th October.

In October 1997 the off-peak Victoria service on weekdays was half-hourly in both directions, with extra trains to London Bridge at peak hours, reducing to an hourly service in the late evenings and on Sundays. The running time to Victoria was 24 minutes, with stops at East Croydon (giving access to fast services to Bedford, Gatwick and the South Coast) and Clapham Junction (for access to Waterloo, the South West and the Continent).

Sanderstead might have been even better connected if a scheme to build a single-track standard gauge light railway from Sanderstead to Orpington was put forward in 1925 by the 'English Light Railway King', Colonel H.F.Stephens had been adopted; it was intended to run via Hamsey Green, Tatsfield, Biggin Hill and Farnborough, and was to be named 'The Southern Heights Light Railway'. SR offered support by offering part of the capital required and an undertaking to carry out the electrification and operation of the line. The scheme eventually foundered when – at the end of 1929 – Colonel Stephens experienced great difficulty in raising his share of the capital, and the original Light Railway Orders lapsed.

The railways have also provided some major alarms. In the early 1970s British Rail mooted plans for two additional tracks for a high speed link to the Channel Tunnel along the route of the Oxted line. The proposal was strenuously opposed, and was finally dropped in 1978 although it briefly twitched its tail in 1986. That was not to be the end of the Chunnel link story so far as Sanderstead was concerned. With its completion delayed until at least nine years after the opening of the Channel Tunnel itself, BR has meantime upgraded tracks and signalling along the Brighton line as far as Redhill, and over the cross-country line to Ashford and Dover to take the heavy freight trains to and from the Continent. In 1995 there was also a private company's proposal to build two additional tracks alongside the existing ones. It aroused vigorous local protests, and was comprehensively defeated when presented to Parliament.

Is rail travel worth it? The single 2nd class fare from Croydon to London in 1839 was 1s. 3d. By 1934 the 3rd class single fare from Sanderstead or Purley Oaks to London was 1s. 7d. and remained so into the early 1940s. In 1996, prior to privatisation, a 2nd class standard single from Sanderstead to London is £4.00. The degree of comfort, safety, speed and reliability has, of course, improved enormously over the intervening years.

Upon privatisation in 1996, the rail services through Sanderstead were taken over by Connex South Central.

Road Transport

In the latter half of the 19th century the railways provided the means of travelling long distances with speed and ease, but further means of transport were necessary if that speed and ease of movement were to spread outwards. The roads were already in place but until the arrival of the bicycle and the internal combustion engine the horse was the only means of moving people and goods across country at other than walking pace.

The villagers of Sanderstead could have seen some of the earliest developments of the new methods of transport, thanks to the proximity of the Brighton Road. 1896 saw the passing of an Act enabling vehicles to travel on the highway at 12 mph without being preceded by a man walking with a red flag. Contemporary photographs show that the bicycle was established in the village by then, the policeman – for one – having exchanged his horse for a staid and sturdy model.

The earliest motor bus route along the Brighton Road appeared in 1905, but it was not until 1921 that the London General Omnibus Company came to an agreement with the East Surrey Traction Company of Reigate regarding the operation of buses in the North Downs area. By that time buses had improved in reliability, had increased in power and were more able to tackle the steep climbs presented by such roads as Sanderstead Hill and Botley Hill. The East Surrey Traction Company, acting as agents for the London General Omnibus Company, began running its blue painted buses through the village on 16th August 1921, to and from West Croydon Station.

The service was an hourly one, the buses running alternately to Sevenoaks and Edenbridge via Botley Hill. For the first three years the route came to Sanderstead by way of the Brighton Road to the *Red Deer*, South Croydon, then up Sanderstead Road. Buses were limited to single-decks by the low railway bridge over Sanderstead Road, but a move was made to remedy this in 1924, when a new service using a double-decker 'K'-type bus was introduced. It was routed to avoid the bridge by travelling from West Croydon via Park Lane, Coombe Road, Carlton Road and Mayfield Road to terminate near Sanderstead Station. The service ran every 40 minutes.

At first there was vocal opposition to the service, which the East Surrey took steps to mollify by placing discs on the wheels of the bus and immaculately painting its bodywork. In addition, the driver was kitted out with a new pair of gloves, and it was said that the ensemble was known locally as 'The Showboat'. The ploy seems to have worked as opposition soon died away, and from 6th October 1924 the original service used the new route, leading in time to the introduction of double-decker buses in place of the single-decks. On 1st December 1924 the services were numbered 403 and 404, but the latter ceased on 15th April 1930. The East Surrey was renamed London General Country Services in 1932.

After World War II, for a while services 408 and 470 ran through Sanderstead from Chelsham to Guildford and Dorking respectively. Service 403 – like an old soldier – has never died, although it has changed its shape, colour and operators over the years, and at the time of writing terminates at the Sainsbury's Supermarket in Warlingham (built on the site of a demolished Country Services garage) with regular extensions to Warlingham Park Hospital. It is operated by London Links, the buses are double-deckers painted in two shades of green, and the service is frequent – during weekdays every 10 minutes for most of the day and every 15 or 30 minutes in early morning and late evening. On Sundays the buses run at 30 minute intervals.

London urban route 234 was initiated in the mid-1930s between Carshalton, Purley and Mitchley Avenue. After 1948 it became a Wallington to Selsdon service, extended from Mitchley Avenue to run along Rectory Park and Addington Road. In the early 1990s it was replaced by the 412 service, operated mainly with single-deck red buses as part of the London Transport system from Norwood Junction Station to Tesco's Supermarket in Purley via central Croydon and Selsdon. In 1997 the buses ran at 15 minute intervals during most of every weekday, the intervals increasing to 30 minutes in early morning and late evening. There was no Sunday service. Selsdon had services 64, 354 and 359, operated by Metrobus in a striking livery of dark blue and yellow, giving frequent buses every day to central Croydon, Forestdale and New Addington, with an hourly weekday extension to Bromley. In 1930 the London General formed Green Line Coaches Ltd. to provide a limited-stop express network through and around London. One of its first services ran hourly through Sanderstead between Oxford Circus and Oxted, with extensions to Edenbridge. The service was routed along Upper Selsdon Road, Addington Road and Limpsfield Road, and lasted until 31st August 1939 when all Green Line services ceased at the imminent outbreak of World War II, not to resume until 1946. By this time the London Passenger Transport Board was in charge. From May 1943 all buses were withdrawn on Sunday mornings as an economy measure – a suspension which lasted until 1946.

When the Green Line coaches returned, they were as services 706 and 707, running hourly from Westerham and Oxted respectively, through Sanderstead to Victoria and Aylesbury in Buckinghamshire. In 1970 London Country Bus Services, a subsidiary of the National Bus Company, took over Green Line Coaches and other country services of London Transport, which included route 403. The writing was on the wall as travel by private cars grew, and soon Green Line coaches were no longer to be seen passing through Sanderstead.

Tilling bus on Sanderstead Hill, c.1921

The same view as above, in 1998, with service no.403

COMMUNICATIONS – MOVING ONTO THE FAST TRACK

Most of the children travelling to and from school by public transport use the usual bus services, but these have been augmented during term-time by two buses in the morning and one in the afternoon, running as route 612 between South Croydon and Wallington via Selsdon, Sanderstead Church, Riddlesdown, Purley and Woodcote. In addition, a 412 double-decker bus has been diverted morning and afternoon along Limpsfield Road and Mitchley Hill to its junction with Mitchley Avenue to serve Riddlesdown High School.

Looking back it can be seen what a crucial role public transport has played in the growth and nature of Sanderstead. Changes were to follow as the motorcar became ever more within the reach of those who hitherto had only public transport available to them. New estates have been built away from established rail and bus routes, and have responded to the rapid expansion of car ownership by providing individual houses with garages or groups of houses with spaces for off-street parking. Large car-parks have been sited near Sanderstead Station and in the centre of the Village, but elsewhere cars are parked by the roadside except where organisations have provided their own parking areas. This state of affairs has led to problems in some roads used as rush hour 'rat-runs'. Compared to most of the older parts of Croydon, the traffic through Sanderstead is relatively free-flowing except for short periods at peak travel times on parts of the main routes.

In the Air

Sanderstead may not have had an airfield set within its boundaries but ever since the siting of military airfields at Kenley, Biggin Hill and Beddington during World War I it has had a grandstand view of the development of international aviation.

In 1920, the airfield at Beddington had grown into Croydon Aerodrome and become the Customs airport for London. By 1929 it had become the busiest airport in Europe. During the 1920s and 1930s all the leading types of transport aircraft belonging to airlines from all over Britain and Europe were to be seen at some time or other on the hardstanding in front of the airport's terminal building, from the flat roof of which the public were able to view all that went on, including the beginning or end of many historic flights.

Sanderstead was under the flight path of many of the aircraft flying to and from the Continent, often at quite low altitudes, but none of them appears to have come to grief within the bounds of the parish. Mrs.Davison, who lived with her family in Selsdon however, had cause for complaint in 1933 when she found some of her washing badly soiled one day after an airliner had flown low over her house. This puzzled her until a friend observed, as an aircraft flew over and she looked up at it, that she should not do that when it was a foreign one as he had flown to Paris recently, and had been horrified to find that when he flushed the toilet it had no container beneath it to collect the waste. Doubly horrified, as her baby was often left in the garden to enjoy the fresh air and sunshine, Mrs.Davison reported the matter to the local Residents' Association and a protest was launched. Subsequently appropriate regulations for all aircraft were issued, and Mrs.Davison felt sure it was as a result of the local protest.

The only civil aircraft known to have crashed in Sanderstead was a de Havilland DH9 belonging to Surrey Flying Services, which was based at Croydon Aerodrome. It was taking part in a film of World War I being made in November 1928. Disguised as a German fighter, it was 'attacked' in a mock dog-fight over Croham Hurst on 17th November but unfortunately crashed into a house, 'Katoomba', in East Hill, the residence of Mrs.Wheeler and Mrs.Carlisle. Both of the ladies were out at the time; the maid, who was working in the cellar and the charlady, who was at the back of the house, were both unhurt. The house was badly damaged and the aircraft was wrecked, ending upside down in the garden, its engine having become detached from the fuselage on impact and flung clear. Although the fuel tank was fairly full there was no fire and Mr. Howells, who was driving Dr.Woolrich nearby in his car at the time, managed to pull the airmen from the aircraft with the aid of neighbours.

The pilot, Captain Frederick Smith, who lived in South Croydon, suffered severe head injuries and remained unconscious for three weeks but recovered to fly again nine months later. His mechanic, Mr. F.A. Kent, from Carshalton, had one of his arms broken but was able to leave Croydon Hospital after treatment.

With so much activity in the airspace around Coydon, it is not surprising that Sir Alan Cobham's Air Display first visited Sanderstead in the early 1930s, and was encouraged to return on 31st August and 1st September 1935. It was Sir Alan's aim to make the British public air-minded and to give impetus to the development of British civil aviation. Seven machines took part in the Display at Sanderstead Park Estate, Limpsfield Road, ranging from a 3-engined Airspeed Ferry, built to Sir Alan's requirements, through single-engined Avro 504s to a Cierva Autogyro. 50 readers of the *Croydon Advertiser* received free flights in the aircraft as guests of Sir Alan and the newspaper, and they were joined by a large number of paying passengers. One lady, who had her free flight in the Autogyro, lost her brand new hat over Selsdon but wrote to the *Advertiser* to tell them that the flight was greatly enjoyed and appreciated. All the aircraft were demonstrated in the air, and the *Advertiser* reported that 'the stunt flying would have satisfied the most exacting seeker after sensation'. A gliding exhibition had been arranged by the newspaper, the pilot being Miss Joan Meakin in a Wolf glider who showed her skill by faultlessly looping the loop three times before landing. There was a parachute drop by Mr J.A.L. Harris, parties of youngsters were given guided tours around the aircraft taking part in the display and the famous midget aeroplane, the 'Flying Flea', was on exhibition but not flown due to the bumpiness of the flying field.

Advertisement for Sir Alan Cobham's Air Display, 1935

COMMUNICATIONS – MOVING ONTO THE FAST TRACK

Just beyond the parish boundary in Hamsey Green, south of Kingswood Lane, was a grass airfield opened in 1933 by Mr. Richard Gardner, managing director of the Yardley Cosmetic Company in London and a resident of Warlingham. He was a keen pilot, and during the 1930s up to 16 light aeroplanes were parked at the airfield at various times, most of them registered to him. One of his sons, Charles Gardner, had learnt to fly with Surrey Flying Services and became one of the best known and successful racing pilots in Britain in the years immediately before World War II. He won his first major air race in 1933 and went on to win the prestigious King's Cup Air Race in 1936 and again in 1937, when he flew his blue-painted Percival Mew Gull, a single-engined low-wing monoplane. After the 1937 Race he was presented with the Cup, and a £1000 first prize, by King George VI in person.

The airfield was closed to civil aircraft at the beginning of World War II, and although occasional RAF aircraft used it during the War, it was not re-opened when peace came. The large hangar was destroyed by fire in 1976 and its concrete floor is now part of the stable-yard of the Kingsmead Equestrian Centre. As for the large flat area of the airfield itself, it has become ideal ground for a variety of sports.

Air ambulance at Sanderstead Recreation Ground 1994

With the coming of war in September 1939 an end was put to all civil flying in Britain for the following six years, and the skies above Sanderstead became the scene of much military activity. At the end of the war, the rapid development in the size and performance of transport aircraft made the runways of Croydon Airport too short for their safe operation and there was no room for expansion. By 1959 only some small airlines and charter companies, together with a few flying clubs, remained at Croydon, and Heathrow had been officially designated London Airport.

Sanderstead's grandstand view of international aviation did not end, however. The parish lies below flight paths to Heathrow, Gatwick, Stansted and Luton Airports. In clear skies, criss-crossing vapour trails can often be seen, marking the passage of over-flying aircraft. It is not unusual for half a dozen or more aircraft to be in view at the same time, at different altitudes and on different flight paths. Although the once-military airfields of Biggin Hill and Kenley have long been closed, the former is still active as a civil airport for executive and light aircraft and brings to the area an impressive array of military and civil aeroplanes, some of them 'vintage', with the air fairs and Battle of Britain commemorations held there each year. Kenley's contribution to the air scene is of the silent kind, with craft of the gliding fraternity often to be seen over Sanderstead, seeking and riding the thermals above Riddlesdown.

The ubiquitous helicopter must not be forgotten. Selsdon Park Hotel has a helicopter pad in its grounds, whilst police and ambulance helicopters have been known to land in the Sanderstead Recreation Ground and on Riddlesdown when emergencies have arisen.

SOURCES

'Bell Street', (1974) *The East Surrey*. H.J. Publications

Bourne Society *Local History Records* and **Bulletins**

CONWAY, D. (1986). The Flying Gardner Family of Hamsey Green. *Aviation News*, 22nd August 1986

CLUETT, D., NASH, J. & LEARMOUTH, B.(1980). *Croydon Airport 1926-39* Sutton Libraries & Arts Services

Croydon Advertiser

Croydon Local Studies Library

Croydon Natural History & Scientific Society (1997) Bulletin No. 103

GLYNNE-JONES, R. (1994). *Purley Downs Golf Club - a Centenary Celebration.* Purley Downs Golf Club.

HALPENNY, B.B. (1984). *Military Airfields of Greater London.* Patrick Stephens

HIBBS, J. (1989). *The History of British Bus Services.* David & Charles

KIDNER, R.W. (1975). *The Oxted Line.* Oakwood Press

MAGGS, K. & DE'ATH, P, (1987) *The Roman Roads of East Surrey and the Kent Border.* North Downs Press.

PHILLIPSON, G. (1988). *The Oxted Line.* Railways of the South East Vol. 1 No. 2

TAYLOR, C. (1979). *Roads and Tracks of Britain.* Dent

WHITE, H.P. (1982) *Regional History of the Railways of Great Britain: Southern England.* David & Charles

Local Directories and Timetables.

Chapter 14

From Village Store to Supermarket

(Shops and Trades)

by Francis Davison

The Old Village on the Hill

As has been mentioned in Chapter 7, during the 19th century Sanderstead village had the basic facilities to support a small agricultural community. There was a village shop, a dairyman, a blacksmith and a wheelwright. These continued in the old village on the hill until the 1930s. Mrs Frosel ran the village shop until 1918, when it was taken over by Stephen Leppard, who carried it on at least until 1927. By the 1930s it passed through the hands of both Smith and Allison. Albert Frost took over the Fox Farm Dairy from his mother, after his father's death in 1899 and continued until 1919 when he sold out to Welford's Surrey Dairies Ltd. Thomas Dulake was the blacksmith until 1911, and was succeeded by Charles Bale. By 1930 Mr Bale's smithy had moved to a building at Borough Farm; the old smithy was a doctor's surgery. By 1937 his son had joined him in the business. James Bex the wheelwright closed his business in about 1898. His son, James Robert, became a carpenter and builder and moved to Croydon. He was responsible for building many houses just outside the parish in the Wyche Grove area, and later became a funeral director.

The Village Shop with the Frosel family *c.*1896

Developments in the north of the Parish: Kensington Place

Whilst the old village changed little during the later decades of the 19th century, building development in other parts of the parish led to the growth of new shopping developments. The first, at Kensington Place, was really part of the growth of South Croydon.

In Sanderstead Road several small houses were converted into, or at least used as, shops. Judging by the short life of most of them they did not prosper. In the 1880s this development crept across the parish boundary, with Kensington Terrace (regarded as amongst the worst housing in Croydon) being within the parish by about a yard. In 1885 three shops, forming Kensington Place, were built, but did not prosper. None was occupied until Mrs Randel opened a greengrocer's at No.1 in 1886. This had closed by 1887. It was succeeded in 1888 by Castle & Co., bootmakers, but again they had gone by 1889. In 1890 William Wood opened a general shop there which continued in business until 1896.

In the meantime, No.2 had remained empty until 1891, when Thomas Ralph opened a draper's shop there. This too continued until 1896. At that time Nos.1 and 2 were taken over by Merrony & Turner, who ran a general store or grocery store, sometime trading as 'The Bazaar'. They continued in business until 1905, after which A.G.Merrony continued until 1911.

No.3 was a little more successful. Alfred Simmons, a retired local policeman, set up as a general dealer in 1886, continuing there until 1897, when he was succeeded by Mrs E. Simmons (presumably his widow), who converted the shop to a confectioner's. She in turn was succeeded by M.E. Simmons, (presumably related) in 1908. He turned the shop into a tobacconist's, but gave it up by 1910, when for a year it was used for a domestic agency by Miss Merrony. She then turned it into a confectioner's. By 1914 it was unoccupied again.

In 1913 A.G.Mason set up a grocer's in Nos.1 and 2, and was still in business in 1937.

In 1915 A.Ede & Sons set up as bootmakers. They are still in business, although they moved three doors north, to the other side of Kensington Terrace, in about 1930.

The Growth of the Building Trade

In 1884 Sanderstead Station was opened, and suddenly the northern part of the parish had access by train to Croydon and, more importantly, to central London. This led to the sale of agricultural land for housing and a steady growth of houses and people. These included both grand individual houses and larger numbers of more modest houses for the middle classes.

The growth of north Sanderstead naturally led to the appearance of members of the various building trades, first as individual tradesmen, later as building firms. The first building tradesmen to be mentioned in Sanderstead in Ward's Directories were William Saker, a bricklayer, and Richard Jenkins, a house carpenter. Both lived in the parish, probably in the old village. Saker was in business in Sanderstead from 1889 to 1901. Richard Jenkins is shown in the records only until 1891. Thomas Bate, another carpenter, is shown from 1894 until 1907, living in Sanderstead Road. In 1909 Thomas Underwood, a plumber, arrived at 2 Norman Cottages, Sanderstead Road, later renamed 12 Purley View, staying in business at least until World War II, though from 1932 he described himself as 'builder'.

The first building firm to be recorded was Webster and Hawkes, which opened an office at 65 Mayfield Road in 1907. This firm was probably building the houses in Mayfield Road at the time, and it is customary for builders to open an office either in one of the houses or in a temporary building on the site. In 1910 the firm moved to offices in Sanderstead Road, just south of the railway bridge on the Brighton line. In 1919 Webster seems to have retired and the firm thereafter traded as H.P. Hawkes. It continued at these premises until after 1934, and played a significant part in the development of the new Sanderstead, including the Old Rectory and Purley Downs Estates on either side of Purley Downs Road, in the late 1920s and early 1930s.

A second builder, Thomas Cleary, appeared in Penwortham Road in 1910, but was gone by the next year. A third, Charles Thomas lasted longer. He arrived at 'Lynmouth' in Purley Oaks Road in 1910 and later moved to

FROM VILLAGE STORE TO SUPERMARKET

Station Parade, Sanderstead Road – above c.1930, below 1997 *(see overleaf)*

'Elesmond' in Beech Avenue. He continued to trade at that address until 1924, although the firm's name by then included 'and Son'.

Various specialist trades and professions associated with construction also appeared as the building boom developed. In 1902 H.R. Houchin, architect, set up offices by the station in Sanderstead Road, though only temporarily. In 1905 A. Wunderlich, electrical engineer, moved into 'Cuyahoga' in Mayfield Road and E.B.Trigg, architect, into 'Leonora' in the same road. In 1910 James E. Tuke, engineer moved to 'Clappersgate', 18 Mayfield Road. In the 1920s a number of lawyers moved into the parish.

The Development of the Shops by Sanderstead Station

The growth of population to the north of the parish led to the appearance of a new shopping area, which became of much greater significance than Kensington Place.

The fortunes of the first shopkeepers varied. Alfred Lye, at No.1 at the north end of the parade, opened in 1901, opening a sub-post office the next year. He seems to have prospered from the start, continuing in business until 1927. From 1912 to 1920 he also ran a fruiterer's at No.3. Other original shopkeepers were less fortunate and most shops changed hands one or more times during their first few years of operation, though in most cases the trade carried on in the shop remained unchanged. In the case of No.5, the fishmonger's, there seem to have been six changes of ownership between 1908 and 1921, with Harrison and Co. alternating with Arthur Ramkin. Among the more successful were Alex Oswald, who started his business as a 'fly proprietor' in Glossop Road in 1909, and opened an office in the newly built No.8 in 1911. By 1913 he was calling himself a 'cab proprietor'. He continued to operate from that office until about 1930.

One of the most important developments – and one that can be regarded as marking the establishment of Station Parade and Station Approach as a significant commercial and shopping area – was the opening of a branch of the London Joint Stock Bank at No.9 in 1911. Through mergers the bank later became the London Joint Stock and Midland Bank and then, about 1925, the Midland Bank. The branch continued there until the 1980s. In 1930 the second bank, Barclays, opened in Station Parade in Nos.12 & 13.

By the time of World War I the pattern of ownership had settled down. In 1916 James Relf opened his nursery in Purley Oaks Road, nearer to the station than to the old village. In 1921 the first garage was opened, the 'Sanderstead Motor Works', owned by G.S.Vellacott and located in Sanderstead Road, just south of the junction with Broomhall Road. It is a garage to this day, although under different ownership.

In about 1928 three additional lock-up shops were built in Station Approach. In 1930 two little shops were built in St Mary's Road, the first occupied by a dry cleaner's. The second about 1932 was the first base of Dick Townley's sports outfitter's, which moved in 1934 to Station Approach, and later to Cranleigh Parade, where it is still to be found.

Shops in Selsdon

In 1925 Costain started to develop its huge estate in Selsdon, and it recognised that local shopping facilities were essential. The first block of five shops, called 'The Broadway', was built in 1926, followed by a second in 1927. In order to enable the new shopkeepers to become established while the population grew, Costain gave the original shopkeepers of each trade an undertaking that they would have no direct competition for a number of years. This was successful in helping the shopkeepers, but local housewives complained that some shopkeepers exploited their monopolies, with high prices and poor quality. It did succeed in getting shops open fairly quickly. By 1928 there were six shops open, the five in 'The Broadway' and the wine shop across Addington Road, on the corner of Old Farleigh Road. These first shops comprised, in addition to the wine shop, a dairy, a butcher, a chemist, a tobacconist and confectioner (which was also the first post office, though only for about a year), and a ladies' hairdresser.

FROM VILLAGE STORE TO SUPERMARKET

By 1930 the number of shops had almost doubled, and there were other businesses as well. All but one of the shops in the second block of 'The Broadway' were occupied. Beyond them was Selsdon Garage and further down Addington Road there was the Sanctuary Tea Garden at what was to become No.151. On the south side of Addington Road, at what was to become No.238, was G.F.King's general stores. A little further – at No.244 – Charles King had his builder's and decorator's business, whilst at No.254 William Cowley had opened the Cowley Nurseries.

Expansion continued. By 1932 the South Suburban Co-op had opened its shop at Nos.152/154 Addington Road, with Miss England's hairdresser's above. By 1934 on the north side of the road Hubbard & Nash opened their paint store, still operating there to this day, and Bowdich & Grant, auctioneers and valuers, had their office in the same building. At No.111 Addington Road, William Bex, descendant of the old wheelwright of Sanderstead, opened an office for his undertaker's business.

Hubbard & Nash's shop, Addington Road

c.1931

Photograph courtesy of Mike Little

By then, on the south side of Addington Road were—

Nos.	158	F.D. Forbes, electrical engineers
	160	Bobbies, milliner's
	184	Barclay's Bank
	186	House agent
	188	Tobacconist
	190	Grocer
	224	China shop
	226	Library
	228	Pastry cook
	230	Selsdon Social Club

By 1937 the south side of Addington Road had filled out still further. A baker's had appeared at No.156. Between Nos.162 and 180 eleven businesses had opened, including a second bank, the Midland. Further down, at No.222 a baker's had opened, while on the north side a grocer's had opened at No.143. At No.147 Cecil Ireland had opened a gentlemen's outfitters.

The Ward's *Purley Directory* for 1939 records the shops and flats of Purley Parade, on the north side of Addington Road, as 'building', while Nos.192-194 and 212-218 are recorded as 'unoccupied'. It is not clear how many of these actually opened by the time World War II started, but by 1956 Selsdon Parade was fully occupied, with ten shops open. Nos.212 to 218 on the south side were also open by then. However, Nos.192 and 194 seem to have been demolished (bombed?), and their site is described as 'building land' in Kent's *Guide to Coulsdon and Purley* of that year.

During the first decade after World War II, Nos.208, 210, 220 and 232 Addington Road were built and occupied and Selsdon Garage was opened at No.230. Since then the last gap in the shops has been filled, with Nos.192 to 206 providing a further eight shops.

By the start of 1939 there were 45 separate retail businesses along Addington Road and the subsequent developments bring the total to about 62, so that it is the largest shopping centre in the area.

Purley Oaks Parade

The next shopping centre to be developed was Purley Oaks Parade, near Purley Oaks Station. This was built about 1928, and originally consisted of seven shops. By 1929 four were open; a greengrocer at No.2, a butcher at No. 3, G.E. Lukey's wine and spirits shop at No.5, and a tobacconist and confectioner at No.7. Nos.1 and 4 had found tenants by 1932. W.H. Smith opened a bookstall at No.8 by 1934, but No.6 was not tenanted until about 1939, when Mack & Mack opened an estate agent's office there. No further shops have been built, and of the original ones only Lukey's was long-lasting. It was replaced by a branch of a multiple chain of wine merchants in the 1970s and the shop is now closed. In 1998, of the original seven, three are empty, including Lukey's. There is a dry-cleaner's, two hairdresser's and a general store.

Purley Oaks Parade, 1998

Response to the 1930s Building Boom

Following the success of the Costain estate in Selsdon, the early 1930s were marked by a rapid growth of housing in several parts of Sanderstead, including the area near the church and old village, Hamsey Green and Riddlesdown. Each of these developments was followed by the building of new shops. By 1934 a start had been made, and the first shops opened in Cranleigh Parade, Hamsey Green Parade and Lower Barn Road. The first two of these Parades grew rapidly and flourished; the third was slow to fill and has remained at its original size.

FROM VILLAGE STORE TO SUPERMARKET

— Cranleigh Parade

Cranleigh Parade consists of four almost identical blocks, each of six shops. They are situated on the east side of Limpsfield Road, opposite the old village shop and school. The three northernmost blocks are separated from the fourth by Cranleigh Gardens. They were all built between 1932 and 1938, and seem to have flourished from the start.

Cranleigh Parade, Limpsfield Road, before 1962

From Cranleigh Parade towards the school on a December day in the 1980s.
Photograph courtesy of Mrs. Serre

Two of the original businesses are still trading under their original names, Gwen Barry, ladies' hairdresser since at least 1934, and E. Seymour, butcher, at least from 1937. Seven other businesses starting in the 1930s lasted at least until the 1960s.

By 1934 all six shops in the first block were let and trading. The second block was also already built by 1934, but only two units were open. By 1937 the remainder had been let, the third block built, and three of its units let too. By 1939 the fourth block had also been completed and all but one of its units let. In 1939 the other three blocks were fully let. The old village shop across the road continued to function as a general store, off-licence and post office.

Since 1939 the parade has changed comparatively little, though the trade carried on in just over half of the shops has changed. Along Limpsfield Road, where Borough Farm stood (used as a riding school in the 1930s) there have appeared a petrol station and a d.i.y. store. However, the 'building land' mentioned in Ward's Directory for 1939 has been turned not into more shops but into a public open space, the 'Gruffy'.

— Hamsey Green Parade

Hamsey Green Parade was built about 1933, at the same time as the first two blocks of Cranleigh Parade and in a fairly similar mock Tudor style. It consisted of two blocks of nine shops each, on the west side of Limpsfield Road, just north of the boundary with Warlingham. Although all 18 shops were built by 1934 only eight were occupied by that time. By 1937 all but one had been let.

Hamsey Green parade – from an old postcard (1936)

FROM VILLAGE STORE TO SUPERMARKET

Hamsey Green shopping centre differs from the others described above in that more than half its present shops were built since World War II. By 1956 there were seven shops on the east side of Limpsfield Road. Since then Kingswood Nurseries, which had been situated just north of Kingswood Avenue have been replaced by a block containing six shops, two big shops at Nos.341/343 and Nos.345/347 have been built, and the Co-op has been developed from a butcher's shop into a supermarket. Just to the south of the shops a garage has been built, just in front of the cottage from which the Bex family ran its wheelwright's business in the 19th century.

Hamsey Green has neither attracted a bank nor even a building society. None of the shops set up before World War II is still in business, and very unusually none of the shops in the two original blocks is still carrying on the same trade as when it opened.

— Lower Barn Road and Mitchley Avenue

The block of five shops on the north side of Lower Barn Road was built at the same time as the first block in Cranleigh Parade and Hamsey Green Parade but it did not share their success. One shop, Hall's newsagent and tobacconist was open by 1934. The other three shops remained unlet at the outbreak of World War II. Today four are occupied by retailers and the fifth by an office.

Another row of five shops serving the growing Riddlesdown estates was built in 1939 in Mitchley Avenue, on the corner of Copthorne Rise. The shops were not fully completed by the outbreak of war and only the newsagent's at the west end of the terrace was open during the war, operating at first from a shed behind the permanent building. After the war the remaining shops soon opened. The second along was a greengrocer, the third a butcher, the fourth a grocer and the fifth a hardware shop. The parade still flourishes, with the newsagent's and the grocer's shop still keeping to their original trades, though under different ownership.

— Limpsfield Road, opposite the former Fire Station

A further shop development just before the outbreak of war was the building of a block of four shops on the west side of Limpsfield Road, just south of the junction with Mitchley Hill. The shops were built in 1939 but only three were completed and occupied by the outbreak of war. They comprised Barber's Stores (a grocer's), Gosden's newsagent's, and a hairdresser's. The fourth, Victoria Wine, opened part time in 1944 as there was not enough stock available to justify full time opening, but it is still in business today. The other shops are still open today but are in the hands of different businesses from those which started there.

In 1939, across Mitchley Hill on the opposite corner was the John Laing estate office. On the corner of Sanderstead Court Avenue, was the newly established Sanderstead Court Garage. The estate office has since been replaced by the Mitchley Hill Service Station and Shop, but the garage across the road is still there, with a car sales business at the front and a separate motor engineering business behind.

— Elmfield Way

A parade of nine shops in three blocks was built in Elmfield Way in about 1958 by A.J.Wait & Co. to serve the new housing on the Fox Farm Estate. The shops were let around 1959 to 1960 and they provide a flourishing and popular shopping centre today. A significant feature of this development was that it was the first shopping parade in Sanderstead that was not directly served by public transport, but had to rely mainly on customers using their private cars. In consequence it was laid out with ample parking space.

The Growth of Shops in Sanderstead and Selsdon

The shopping facilities of Sanderstead and Selsdon have grown following closely the increase of new housing so that there is now a wide range of facilities to meet local needs despite the proximity of shops in Croydon and, in recent years, the appearance of large supermarkets on Purley Way, in Purley and in Warlingham. However, the pattern is continuing to change. Proximity to a railway station is now much less important than it was. Easy, and preferably free, parking is of increasing importance. The proposed introduction of charges for parking at Selsdon and at Sanderstead Station may well have an adverse effect on these two centres.

The pattern of development of the different shopping centres is summarised in the table below.

The Changing Pattern of Shopping Centres in Sanderstead and Selsdon

DISTRICT	1880	1914	1939	1956	1997
Old Village, Limpsfield Rd	1	1	28	33	25
Sanderstead Station		15	19	18	11
Selsdon			38	50	43
Purley Oaks			9	9	5
Hamsey Green			17	23	20
Riddlesdown			1	10	9
Elmfield Way					9
Total	1	16	112	143	122

Note: The above figures cover shops, including such retail services as hairdressing and dry cleaning. They exclude banks, builders, building societies, estate agents, garages, insurance brokers, pubs, restaurants and take-aways. In each case the figures are those at the start of the year.

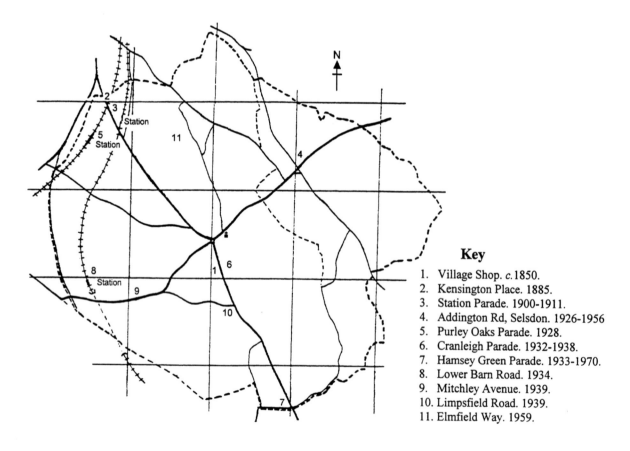

Key

1. Village Shop. *c.*1850.
2. Kensington Place. 1885.
3. Station Parade. 1900-1911.
4. Addington Rd, Selsdon. 1926-1956
5. Purley Oaks Parade. 1928.
6. Cranleigh Parade. 1932-1938.
7. Hamsey Green Parade. 1933-1970.
8. Lower Barn Road. 1934.
9. Mitchley Avenue. 1939.
10. Limpsfield Road. 1939.
11. Elmfield Way. 1959.

DEVELOPMENT OF SHOPS IN SANDERSTEAD AND SELSDON

Changes in the Types of Shop and Other Business

As well as growing, and occasionally shrinking in particular areas, the trades represented in Sanderstead and Selsdon have changed quite a lot over the years. The table below summarises the numbers in twenty categories at four different dates.

The Changing Distribution of Trades in Sanderstead and Selsdon

Trade	1914		1939		1956		1997	
	No.	%	No.	%	No.	%	No.	%
Grocers & general stores	6	23	16	11	21	12	9	5
Greengrocers & florists	1	4	7	5	13	7	9	5
Butchers & fishmongers	2	8	11	7	13	7	2	1
Bakers & cake shops	-	-	5	3	7	4	3	2
Newsagents, confectioners & tobacconists	2	8	16	11	21	12	15	9
Chemists & opticians	1	4	7	5	9	5	10	6
Drapers, clothing & needlework	1	4	14	10	15	8	12	7
Hardware & d.i.y	1	4	7	5	13	7	18	11
Shoes & shoe repairs	1	4	3	2	5	3	1	1
Wine merchants & off-licences	-	-	3	2	5	3	8	5
Estate & insurance agents & solicitors	2	8	10	7	7	4	15	9
Pubs, cafés, restaurants & take aways	-	-	6	4	5	3	14	8
Electrical, gas, TV & radio	-	-	2	1	7	4	4	2
Nurserymen	1	4	6	4	4	2	1	1
Banks & building societies	1	4	5	3	5	3	8	5
Hairdressers	-	-	10	7	10	6	14	8
Garages & petrol stations	-	-	4	3	7	4	10	6
Laundries & dry cleaners	-	-	1	1	5	3	4	2
Other shops	1	4	4	3	3	2	3	2
Other services	6	23	11	7	5	3	10	6
Total	26		148		180		170	

Postal Services

The Post Office is Britain's oldest nationalised industry. The General Post Office was founded in 1710, the successor to earlier institutions dating back to the Middle Ages, but until the early 19th century it touched Sanderstead very little. The nearest Post Office was in Croydon. Letters had to be delivered to and collected from the office, and the fee was payable by the recipient. Receiving a letter was a rare and expensive event. The Sanderstead Churchwardens recorded the cost of letters as a separate item in their accounts. They received three

A HISTORY OF SANDERSTEAD

in 1795, but only one in 1790, 1794, 1796 and 1798. In the early 19th century, the 'London Twopenny Post' was set up, covering Sanderstead and the other parishes south of Croydon, with a receiving office in Warlingham.

The big step forward was the introduction of the penny post throughout the country in 1840. The price of posting a letter dropped by over 83% and the postage was now paid by the sender when buying a stamp. This made it possible for ordinary people to use the postal service. The new service extended to Sanderstead, but facilities grew only slowly. By 1851 there was a daily delivery at 8 a.m. to Miss Maria Ellen Coombe, the schoolmistress, and a daily collection at 3 p.m. It was not until 1870 that the first pillar box was erected in the village and 1890 before the village shop became a sub post office. The second sub-post office was opened at 1 Station Parade in 1902 to meet the needs of the growing lower village and by 1912 there were some eight post boxes and nine collections a day.

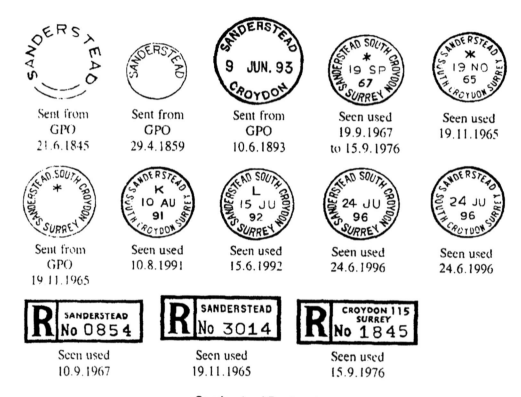

Sanderstead Postmarks

The great building boom of the late 1920s and 1930s brought further developments. The first sub post office in Selsdon opened in 1927. In 1934 post offices were opened in Lower Barn Road and Hamsey Green and the most recent was opened in Elmfield Way in 1960. The ownership and location of the post offices has changed at intervals but the overall pattern of five sub-post offices remains and Sanderstead still has no main post office.

SOURCES

Churchwardens' accounts for Sanderstead Parish

Information supplied by A.F. Moyles and K. Harman

Surrey and Croydon Trade Directories

Chapter 15

Churches and Chapels

by Margaret Isted Osborn

Before the 20th century, the spiritual life of Sanderstead was centred around All Saints' Church, which for over seven centuries has been at the centre of the village and at its highest point. The building has been altered many times during its life, both inside and out, but many of its original features remain. There has been continuity of worship there since its earliest days, including throughout the troubled times of the Reformation, the Civil War and Commonwealth. Today's residents still enter through the same oak door as their forefathers did in the 13th century. Much of the church's early history has been referred to in opening chapters of this book.

Since the Reformation until the 20th century denominations other than Anglican had no place of their own within the parish. The population of Sanderstead had been growing steadily since the opening of Sanderstead Railway Station in 1884 and Purley Oaks Station in 1899, and at the turn of the century was just over 1000.

The 1895 Ordnance Survey Map of South Croydon shows a **Salvation Army** Barracks in Bynes Road which would have drawn people living in Sanderstead. The barracks, which could hold 40 people, was situated in Coopers Crescent, where John Cooper (Boot and Shoe Manufacturers) had built a colony of houses (Nos. 103-183 Bynes Road) for some of his outworkers.

St. Gertrude's Church, built 1906.   *Photo 1997.*

Located just inside the boundary of South Croydon, the first modern church to be built was **St Gertrude's**, at the corner of Wyche Grove and Purley Road, built with money left by Miss Frances Ellis to the Roman Catholic Diocese. It was opened as a mission in June 1903. The cost, including the presbytery, was just under £3000. The eastern boundary to be served ran from the south-east end of Riddlesdown where the District Council boundary cuts the Godstone Road, and follows this boundary going north-east to Addington Lodge. The mission was upgraded to a parish in 1920. In World War II, on 11th May 1941, the Church suffered the effects of a bomb when one side was damaged and the organ and gallery were destroyed. Two masses were said before the Church was ordered to evacuate and services were moved to St. Anne's Convent for three weeks whilst the building was made safe. Mention must be made of Father Pritchard who was rector in charge at St. Gertrude's for over 25 years. It was under his guidance that four new churches were established, including the Church of the Holy Family in Sanderstead. When he used to pay the weekly collection into the bank he was often ribbed about the

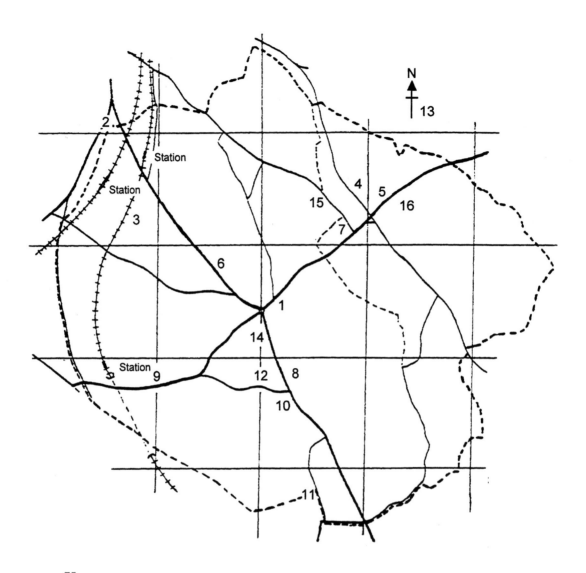

Key

1. All Saints' Parish Church. 1230.
2. St. Gertrude's Roman Catholic Church. 1903.
3. St. Mary's Church. 1908.
4. Catholic Church of St. Columba. 1926.
5. Selsdon Baptist Church. 1927.
6. Sanderstead United Reformed Church. 1903.
7. St. John's Church, Selsdon. 1936.
8. Church of the Holy Family. 1951.
9. St. Edmund's Church. 1954.
10. Sanderstead Methodist Church. 1955.
11. St. Antony's Church. 1957.
12. Mitchley Hill Chapel. 1957.

**PLACES OF WORSHIP
IN SANDERSTEAD AND
SELSDON**

small-denomination coins, which took some time to check. A reading room was named in memory of him at St.Gertrude's.

The interior of St. Gertrude's Church (from an old postcard)

Photo: Grahame Brooks

St. Anne's Convent was opened on 12th September 1909 by six nuns of the Ladies of Mary from the community at Coloma, Shirley. It was in the chapel of this school that mass was said for the first time in Sanderstead for over 300 years. In 1980 – in the 71st year of its foundation – St. Anne's closed and amalgamated with Coloma R.C. Girls School – back to the community from which St. Anne's had originated. The grounds of St. Anne's were soon developed for housing, but the wall and railings in Sanderstead Road have been left intact and on the gates the insignia of the Ladies of Mary can still be seen. A Bourne Society plaque to commemorate the school can also be seen there. The unveiling of the plaque, on 26th July 1996, was attended by a large crowd, including 93 years old Miss Skinner, who was one of the first pupils.

With the increased housing development at the lower end of Sanderstead it was decided to make provision for a separate Anglican mission church for people who wished to worship nearer to their own homes. In 1908 **St. Mary's Church** was opened by the Bishop of Southwark in a temporary building in Purley Oaks Road on land generously donated by Mr Arkwright of the Arkwright Estate. This original building still serves as St. Mary's Church Hall. The cost of the building was £665. An extension was added in 1915 and at the same time plans were made to build a permanent church. Fund-raising was started, but with the hardship after World War I the work on the new church did not commence until 21st July 1925 and by this time the original estimate had doubled. Plans were altered, economies had to be made, and fund raising efforts were organised yet again. The completion of the Church was marked by a Service of Dedication on 25th February 1971 in the presence of the Bishop of Woolwich, the Right Revd. D S Sheppard MA.

St. Mary's Church, Beech Avenue/Purley Oaks Road. Photographed in 1997

Sanderstead in the 1930s was still a rural area, but with people walking to the stations each day to catch trains for town. The view from the top of Purley Downs Road was open; Millers Farm was on the corner on the left with glebe lands behind it. Up to this time lavender had been cultivated in the fields alongside the lane which was later to become Sanderstead Hill, supplying the Mitcham trade for many years. Against this setting five men – Herbert Fisher, J Rowland Hooff, Maldwyn Johnes, Percival Newman and A Emrys Owens – decided in 1931 that it was time for Sanderstead to have its own Nonconformist Church. The first Sunday evening services were held at the Sanderstead Memorial Hall, Purley Oaks Road. In February 1932 a site on Sanderstead Hill had been purchased, and in 1933 the foundation stones of **Sanderstead Congregational Church** were laid. In June the following year the first stage of the building was officially opened by the Lord Mayor of London, Sir Charles Collett. The buildings, including the hall, were completed in May 1939. In September of that year the new hall – barely used – was taken over by the army, resulting in all the meetings having to be held in the deacons' vestry or in the transept of the church. Sunday services continued, and at one time the evening service was held under the stage – an area which the Irish Guards were using for storing meat! It was not until 1946 that the premises were handed back to the church.

Women were actively involved at the church from the start, with a working party busy in 1933 raising money for church funds. During the war a canteen was set up for soldiers and a knitting circle was formed. In 1969 No.14 Beechwood Road was purchased by the Church, and Abbeyfield Housing Association was started to provide a home for the elderly within the security and companionship of a small household. In 1975, with the support and interest of friends at St Gertrude's, it was possible to buy a further property at No.2 Beechwood Road.

In 1972 when the Congregational and Presbyterian Churches joined to become the **United Reformed Church**, the Sanderstead Congregational Church voted to become part of this Union.

Sanderstead Congregational Church Ladies' Committee May 1933
Left to right – Back Row – Mrs M. Mason, Mrs Muriel Chesney, Mrs Kathleen Owens,
Mrs Doris Figgis (Wife of the Minister), Mrs Mabel Fisher.
Front Row – Mrs Ethel Newman, Mrs Muriel Johnes, Mrs Edith Hooff.

In 1936 an extension to **All Saints' Church** was built along the whole of the north side, with a Lady Chapel at the east end. Four carved stone heads were incorporated representing the then rector, Howard Rose, two churchwardens – Messrs Dew and Ryde – and the architect of the extension, Mr Tolhurst. The inspiration for this came from the medieval masons whose faces peer down from the pillars in the old nave. This was not the first alteration to the church. Much earlier, during the 18th and 19th centuries, the building had been considerably changed – for example the south side originally had an upper row of windows. It is believed that there was once also a gallery, although no illustrations of the interior in former times have come to light. Many will, however, remember the Victorian decoration whereby winged angels holding texts in their hands adorned the walls of the nave and the chancel arch.

All Saints' Church Choir in 1950

**Raising funds to extend All Saints' Church to celebrate
its 750th Anniversary in 1980**

CHURCHES AND CHAPELS

Until the break-up of the estate in 1919, the advowson of the Church (the right to appoint the rector) was in the possession of the Atwood family and its descendants the Wigsells and Arkwrights. It was sold in 1929 to the Revd. P E Warrington, who lodged it with the Martyrs' Memorial Fund. When the Church Council heard of this in 1934 they took the right of compulsory purchase provided by recent legislation and then placed the 'patronage' in the hands of the Diocese of Southwark, where it remains today.

Considerable damage was done during World War II when the church roof was set ablaze during an air-raid. Due to the prompt action of the rector, parishioners and the fire brigade the damage was contained and the church continued to be used for services despite the inconvenience of the occasional shower! In 1980 a further extension was added to the north of the Lady Chapel to accommodate the increasing number of worshippers. This extension is dedicated to St Catherine, linking it to the earlier chapel of the same name recorded in the will of Dyones Atwood in 1530 (see Chapter 4).

**Bishop Howard Tripp unveiling the
Bourne Society plaque**

During World War II, with the increased travel restrictions, it was decided to provide a place for Roman Catholics to gather for Sunday mass in the village. Two ladies – Miss Richardson and Miss Cox – offered a schoolroom in their kindergarten, 'The Skep', 117 Limpsfield Road as a mass centre. This building had originally been the village smithy. The parish priest was willing to use this room provided he could count on 30 people attending. Mass was said for the first time in November 1942 with 41 people present. When Miss Richardson and Miss Cox retired after the war the land and premises were bought by the Roman Catholic Diocese of Southwark and in 1951 the mission church became known as **The Church of the Holy Family**. It soon became clear that a larger building was required, and in December 1956 a new church was opened with the old smithy as the parish hall. The smithy is over 200 years old – a fact commemorated by a Bourne Society blue plaque. This also records that, in 1992, Bishop Howard Tripp, a member of a well known Sanderstead family and assistant Bishop in the R C diocese of Southwark, celebrated the 50th anniversary of the first mass to be held here.

The foundation stone of **St. Edmund's Church**, Riddlesdown, was laid on 25th September 1954 by Mr John Laing. Up to the outbreak of World War II people from the Laing estate, Riddlesdown, had to walk to All Saints' Church for worship. The curate, Revd. F B Hutchingson, arranged for a private bus to transport the older children to Sunday school, while the younger ones met at the house of Mrs Gibson in Buttermere Gardens. When the wooden estate office at the corner of Mitchley Avenue and Buttermere Gardens became vacant in 1939 permission was sought to use it for the Sunday school. With only a 'Valor' lamp for heating, chairs had to be bought and an old piano acquired. The estate office quickly became a religious and social centre for the community, with Sunday evening services and youth activities. The usage soon outgrew the building, and under the leadership of Mr Goddard (who had previously opened his house to 'The Pilgrim Band' children) the community set about raising funds to build a church of its own. In 1945 Mr Goddard approached Mr John Laing, who offered a site free of charge with the stipulation that the patronage should be in the hands of an evangelical trust. This condition could not be met as responsibility for worship would have had to rest with the rector of Sanderstead. After many discussions Mr Laing renewed his offer of a site without any conditions, and work was started on the building of a combined church and hall.

The Methodist church was also shortly to be represented in Sanderstead and in June 1948 the Croydon quarterly meeting took its first steps. Difficulty was experienced in obtaining planning permission to build in Limpsfield Road, which was at first refused. In 1949 representations were made to the Ministry of Town and Country Planning, and eventually permission was granted. The price of the land was fixed at the very reasonable sum of £100 because under war-time legislation pre-war use was the determining factor. This reflects the relatively low value of farm land at that time. Cows once grazed where the car park now stands! Work commenced on **Sanderstead Methodist Church**, Limpsfield Road, as a dual-purpose building and the foundation stone was laid on 5th March 1955. The ceremony had to be cut to a minimum owing to a snowstorm. The opening service and dedication took place on 1st October 1955, the cost of the building being £16,300.7s. 6d. In 1997 the Cheshire Foundation Housing Association built homes on the land adjacent to the church, specifically for people using wheelchairs, funded mainly by the association, with an additional grant from the local council.

St. Antony's Church, Wentworth Way, was built in 1957 to serve parishioners living in Hamsey Green. Like St. Edmund's, Riddlesdown, it has its own vicar but is part of the team ministry of the parish of All Saints'. The dedication is to one of the early desert fathers, honoured for their wisdom and the sound advice they gave to all who came to them for help.

St. Antony's Church, Hamsey Green.

Revd. David Haywood

1998

In 1958 the **Mitchley Hill Chapel**, Limpsfield Road, was opened at a cost of £9250, an independent evangelical church originally without a minister and bearing no denominational name. It was intended that it would be run by elders. The need for a chapel had been voiced by local residents five years previously, and the eventual building could seat 200 people. As the church fellowship strengthened over the years the members felt able to call on the services of a pastor, and as a body makes a significant contribution to the local community.

Above is a brief history of the development of churches in the Sanderstead area, each begun or enlarged as the need arose. Today there is a strong ecumenical movement, as each one shares in 'Churches together in Sanderstead.'

SOURCES

Church and chapel guides.

Chapter 16

Aspects of Social Life

by Vernon Briggs, Olive Carroll, Ted Frith, Joy Gadsby & John Hewett-Hicks

Walking

Walking is still one of the most popular forms of recreation and Sanderstead is blessed with open spaces, not only the ancient King's Wood, but thanks to the foresight and dedication of earlier residents also:

— Croham Hurst, Upper Selsdon Road

In 1898 the Whitgift Foundation Governors, the owners, proposed selling the wooded lower slopes of Croham Hurst for housing. This was vigorously opposed by local residents and eventually, in 1901, the whole site was sold to Croydon Corporation.

Most of Croham Hurst – the westernmost outcrop of a range of Thanet sands capped with Blackheath pebble beds – lies within the parish of Sanderstead. The geology gives rise to an interesting range of habitats, with steeply wooded slopes and an open heathy plateau.

At the back of the houses on the lower end of Farley Road, still mainly in Sanderstead, is the small Thrift Wood, which is part of Croham Hurst Golf Course. Earlier it was known as Frith Wood and such-named woods are often found on the boundary of a parish (witness the nearby Frith Wood on the border of Farleigh). Frith is a pre-Norman Conquest word, but the old Sussex dialect word 'frith' referred to scrubby woodland where the wood was too young for coppicing.

Walkers (and their canine companions) enjoying a stroll along the main ride in King's Wood, 1997

— Purley Beeches, Beech Avenue

Purley Beeches was planted some time after 1834, on open land forming part of Purley Downs. This is another area saved from development, purchased by local subscription in 1907. 30 years later a plot of adjoining land that had originally belonged to Purley Farm was purchased for £1289. 12s. 0d, raised by 561 supporters including the Archbishop of Canterbury, Eric Wettern, Malcolm Sharpe and Francis Moir.

— Sanderstead Recreation Ground, Limpsfield Road

Sanderstead Recreation Ground was first acquired in 1895, on a 21-year lease at £10 a year rent, from the Trustees of the Arkwright Estate. The newly-elected Parish Council had asked for a piece of flat land near the centre of the village for use as a cricket pitch and undertook the cost of levelling it and sowing the grass. The total cost of the project, for carting, levelling, seeding, and the purchase of a roller and a mower from Hammond & Hussey of Croydon, amounted to £35. 1s. 8d! Today there is not only a cricket pitch but football pitches, a bowling green and a small play area for young children. A fireworks display is held there every year on or near Guy Fawkes' Day.

— Sanderstead Plantation, Addington Road

Finally – in 1933 – the then Coulsdon & Purley Council purchased Sanderstead Plantation.

— The Gruffy, Limpsfield Road/Onslow Gardens

The area known as the Gruffy – a dialect word from lead-mining in Somerset and inferring humpy-bumpy ground – also narrowly escaped development, first for a hospital and later for a car park. Happily it has survived as a public open space.

Cricket

It is known that cricket was played in Sanderstead over 250 years ago. Some of the earliest examples of an organised game took place locally and several matches are known to have been played in the 18th century – at Coulsdon in 1731 and Addington in 1743. The *Postboy* of 8th September 1731 contains a report of an eleven of Surrey meeting an eleven of Middlesex at Sanderstead Common, and on Monday 26th June 1732 another newspaper reported a meeting at Sanderstead Downs, between teams from London and Surrey. It was also reported that there were several very considerable wagers laid upon the game.

The commonly held belief is that the local club was founded in about 1881 during the time that the Cowdrey family, ancestors of the Kent and England cricketer Colin Cowdrey and known to be lovers of cricket, were living at White House Farm. It seems likely that matches were played by teams from the farms. The character of the area began to change with the opening of Sanderstead Station in 1884, and the housing developments around the station brought a much higher population into Sanderstead. One attempt to start a formal cricket club was made as a result of the first meeting to be held in the new Brand Memorial Hall in 1895. For many years a great standby of the team was Bill Bate, a fast bowler; he married one of the Cowdreys.

Tom Sherlock joined the club in 1901 and his name is synonymous with Sanderstead Cricket Club, as a player, captain, benefactor and trustee of the Trust which he formed to ensure that cricket be played in perpetuity in Sanderestead. The club proceeded in a steady, if unspectacular fashion until the outbreak of World War I but the next available records in 1923 show only the name of Tom Sherlock who had played prior to 1914. After the war the club experienced problems and as more and more people were using the recreation ground the cricket pitches were poor. However, in 1921 Tom Sherlock purchased 'The White House', the meadow and the saw mill. He later sold 'The White House' but kept the meadow as a cricket field which is still used by the club today. Prior to 1939 the club played local cricket and this tradition was carried into the post war period. Only in 1970 did the first vestiges of league cricket appear. Sanderstead gained entry into the Surrey County League in 1982 and now competes in the Surrey Championship.

Golf

Sanderstead boasts three golf clubs – Purley Downs, Croham Hurst and Selsdon Park.

Purley Downs Golf Club is situated some 500 feet above sea level, with magnificent views over London, from Windsor Castle and Heathrow Airport in the west, past Hampstead Heath, the Telecom Tower and Crystal

SANDERSTEAD CRICKETERS 1981. Back row: R. Eccles, G. Gord, K. Harrison, K. Haynes, P. Brown (Club Captain), A. O'Sullivan, H. Sherlock, A. Witchell and D. Dennis; Front row: P. Mathews, M. Corderoy, R. Chatham, I. Witchell (Vice-captain), J. Harding (Scorer) and J. Eastwood.
Photo - courtesy Sanderstead Cricket Club

Purley Downs Golf Course   Photographed in 1998

Palace to Canary Wharf in the east. The 90-year old clubhouse stands directly behind the first tee; the spectator has a dramatic view of every shot on this famous downhill par-three, and a restful panorama of the wooded slopes beyond.

Golf was first played on the Downs in the early 1890s, when a group of professional men living in the district caught the wave of enthusiasm for the game spreading southwards from Scotland and persuaded a tenant farmer to let them knock a ball about among his sheep. The fine downland turf and the sweeping natural contours made it an ideal location. Soon nine holes were laid out, a wooden clubhouse built, and in 1900 a lease was agreed with the landlord, the Arkwright Estate. Before long, increasing demand prompted better provision and in 1903-04 an 18-hole course was designed by J.H.Taylor, five times winner of the Open Championship, and a substantial new clubhouse built.

In those early days there were three holes on the west side of the Oxted railway line which were reached by a wooden footbridge across the deep cutting. Sparks from steam engines sometimes burnt the bridge down and an alternative route via the road had to be used. In the 1920s, after the Arkwright Estate was sold, the Club bought the freehold, including several acres on the eastern side which enabled it to sell off the western holes. Purley Downs Golf Club is now a limited company with 2000 shares, the majority of which are owned by the Club itself – a guarantee that golf will continue to be played there in the future.

Selsdon Park was acquired by Alan Doble Sanderson in 1924 and the house converted into an hotel. What he also did, as part of his ambitious plans for the hotel, was to build a golf course in the 200 acre grounds. Even today there are very few full-sized courses attached to hotels. Like Purley Downs, the course was laid out by J.H. Taylor and remains much the same to this day. As a club it closed in 1986 and the course reverted to the sole use of the hotel and its guests.

The entrance to Selsdon Park Golf Club
– from an old postcard.

Tennis

Sanderstead Lawn Tennis Club was founded in 1904 to provide recreational facilities for the residents of the Kendall Estate – one of the first housing developments. During the years up to World War II the club enjoyed a reputation for being somewhat up-market. The Australian Davis Cup Team practised there and in the records is a photograph of the 1932 team at the club. The annual club championships were often umpired by Wimbledon officials.

When Dr. Kendall died in 1961 the owners were keen to develop the site but assisted by a mortgage the club bought the property. However, amenities by then were poor and interest flagged, so that in the early 1970s the club nearly expired. The spur to survive was the threat by the local council to build social housing on the site and local residents rallied round to keep the club going.

The club now prospers with six hard courts, including two carpet courts, a full-time coach, and 300 members with flourishing junior, bridge, table tennis and social sections. The local Sanderstead Junior School also uses the facilities.

The Tennis Club associated with the United Reformed Church was founded in 1933, with play at first on the courts in Carlton Road, South Croydon. The ground in Farm Fields was purchased and an official opening held in 1936 with a grand demonstration and exhibition by the Wimbledon champions, Dorothy Round and Bunny Austin, and the Davis Cup players Phyllis Konstam and H.G.N. Lee. Today the club is still thriving and its membership reflects its strength as there are waiting lists for both junior and senior sections.

Sanderstead Village Lawn Tennis Club was also founded before World War II and is still flourishing.

Badminton

Three badminton clubs exist – one associated with the United Reformed Church, another is based in the hall of All Saints' Church, and St. Antony's, Hamsey Green, hosts the third.

Other sports catered for at Sanderstead Recreation Ground are **Bowls** – for both men and women players – and **Hockey**.

Gardening

Gardening has a wide following in Sanderstead. There is an Allotment Society, based on land at the back of houses in Purley Oaks Road, and two horticultural societies, the White House and the Sanderstead Horticultural Societies. The latter originated from the 'Dig for Victory' Show held in the garden of Sir Richard Manktelow at 21 West Hill on 13th September 1941. Owing to its success and the need to grow vegetables to support the wartime diet, a public meeting was held and a society formed. It became affiliated to the Royal Horticultural Society in 1942, and in 1945 was awarded a bronze medal for apples at the RHS Fruit and Vegetable Show. In 1953 the Sanderstead Horticultural Society's Summer Show was held at 'Roselands', the garden of Eric Wettern who was the Society's President in 1954. When Mr. Wettern presented the garden to the Borough of Croydon to become a public open space he stipulated that the Society should be permitted to continue to hold its annual show there for as long as it wished. In 1962 the Society hosted the BBC Radio Show 'Gardeners' Question Time'. Today it has a large and enthusiastic membership after nearly 60 years. The White House Horticultural Society, though younger, is also strong.

Sanderstead Literary Society

In 1934 enterprising members of the newly instituted Congregational Church (as it was then) formed an organisation to provide evenings of entertainment, interest and discussion. Its title was then 'The Sanderstead Congregational Church Literary and Debating Society' and the subscription for the season of 12 winter evenings was 2s. 6d. It went from strength to strength and generated much interest, attracting people from the surrounding area as well as church members. Only the war years interrupted the momentum but activities continued when hostilities ceased.

Today the Society maintains the high standard that was set so many years ago, although there have of course been many changes, one being the title. It is now called simply 'Sanderstead Literary Society', although it is still very much an organisation of the Sanderstead United Reformed Church. The format has changed over the years from being quite formal to its present rather more relaxed attitude.

Many celebrities have lectured to the Society in the past, including such well known personages as Edgar Lustgarten, Godfrey Talbot, Jack Warner, Roy Plomley, Nicholas Parsons, Jean Metcalfe, Henry Sandon and Antony Hopkins to name just a few. The seasons' programmes cover a variety of subjects, as diverse as London's Lord Mayors, Bridges, SS *Great Britain*, An American View of the British, the theatre and musical entertainments. Wildlife talks and travelogues have also been popular.

Dramatics

Sanderstead Dramatic Society was formed in 1907 and had an enthusiastic following, with regular performances three or four times a year, broken only by the two world wars, when activities had to be suspended. Today it is less active than it was in earlier times but still produces a pantomime every year, which is enjoyed by young and old.

More recently the Parlour Players has been formed, under the auspices of the United Reformed Church, producing a wide range of plays to a very high standard.

SANDERSTEAD DRAMATIC CLUB - JUNIOR SECTION

Sue White   Peter Simpson   Priscilla Wright   ?   Kate Beckley   ?   Brenda Jones   John Page

Sally Hunt   ?Simpson   Pamela Headen   ?

Women's Organisations

By the 20th century the progressive women in this country were seeking more independence and opportunities to educate themselves. They were beginning to air their opinions on matters which concerned them, especially those connected with family life.

Families tended to be smaller and the women wanted a better quality of life and health for their children. This is possibly why the idea of the Women's Institute Organisation (founded in Canada in 1897) was welcomed in this country. The first WI in the United Kingdom was formed in 1915 in Llanfair PG, Anglesey under the auspices of the Agricultural Organisation Society. The members pledged that their Institute would become a 'centre for good in the village'. In 1917 the National Federation of Women's Institutes was formed; by 1919 it was self-governing and there were 1405 Women's Institutes in England and Wales.

Mrs Cecilia Muckelroy, Convenor of the Purley Group Women's Institute, planting a tree in the Wettern Tree Garden, Sanderstead, to celebrate 100 years of the W.I, which was founded in Canada in 1897. The tree planted – *Acer pennsylvanicum* (Moose Bark Maple) – was most appropriate.

Originally the formation of WIs was limited to communities where the number of inhabitants did not exceed 4000, i.e. country villages. However, populations in the rural areas expanded and this rule was rescinded in 1965, thereafter WIs sprang up in small towns, outer suburbs of cities – in fact wherever there was felt to be a need.

Such an organisation for women gave them friendship and opportunities to learn from one another and improve their skills and talents to the benefit of their families.

Sanderstead must have been abreast of the times as a local afternoon Institute was formed as early as 1921 and as the population increased so additional institutes were formed –

1954   Hamsey Green –formerly Evening now Afternoon
1958   Sanderstead Village Evening
1964   Purley Beeches

Purley Beeches has now disbanded but the other groups are still in existence and flourishing, although as younger women are now part of the workforce, most of the members are in the older age bracket.

The Townswomen's Guild is another organisation with similar ideals. One of the forerunners of the TWG was the Kensington Society formed in 1865 – a group of women dedicated to higher educational opportunities for women. When in 1928 franchise on the same terms as men was granted, it raised the problem of how best to educate women to fulfil the responsibility and privilege of full citizenship. In consequence the first Townswomen's Guild was formed in 1929.

Just prior to World War II there was an enormous housing development in the area of Riddlesdown and another one in the 1950s on what had been the Fox Farm Estate. This brought an influx of many young families into the area and prompted the formation of groups to bring the inhabitants together.

The Townswomen's Guild was introduced into the area and the following groups formed –

1956 - Purley & Riddlesdown Evening, now based at St. Edmund's Church Hall, Riddlesdown
1958 - Purley & Riddlesdown Afternoon, also based at St. Edmund's
1962 - Sanderstead Evening, based at the Ridgeway School on the Fox Farm Estate

All these groups are still in existence.

Sanderstead is well served by churches of different denominations – 10 in all. These over the years had and still have various groups to cater for the ladies of their congregations, operating under varying names. One group, Coffee Roundabout, is unique. It was founded in 1966 under the auspices of All Saints' Church, but open to all denominations or none. It meets twice, sometimes three times a month, with a wide range of interesting speakers on topical subjects, crafts, travel etc. The inspiration for the group arose from the need to link young wives from the new housing developments with the older established part of the parish and its success is largely due to its method of organisation. The organiser and treasurer provide continuity but it has a committee structure that rotates on a regular six months' (approx.) basis, thus giving every member an opportunity of being involved in the running of the Society. As with other women's groups, members now tend to be in the older age range. The link formed between 'old' and 'new' Sanderstead in its early beginnings has remained and continues to play an important part in the life of the parish as a whole.

A Floral Arrangement Group for ladies was formed in 1959 and is affiliated to the Sanderstead Horticultural Society.

For its size and population Sanderstead offers ladies, in particular, many opportunities to make friendships and further their education in many ways.

Youth

All the local churches have their own Sunday schools and youth groups and the uniformed organisations are well represented. The first scout troop was established by 1916 but lapsed as numbers of children in Sanderstead

Sea Rangers at camp – 1946

**Cubs, Scouts, Brownies and Guides with the Revd. Howard Rose in the Rectory garden.
Scoutmaster Eric Bishop.   1939.**

dwindled. It was in 1937 that Scouts and Guides started up again in earnest and younger children also clamoured to join, so that Cub Scouts and Brownies, and more recently Beavers and Rainbows are today all active in Sanderstead. Senior Scouts and Rangers have fluctuated more, affected by the fact that many of our young people move away to University. A Sea Ranger crew, SRS *Furious* existed in Sanderstead from 1935 but lapsed before World War II. It was restarted in 1943 by Miss Beatrice Rivet and flourished for nearly 50 years, closing down in 1988. Today there are Scout and Guide units, associated with All Saints', St. Mary's, United Reformed and St. Gertude's churches, as well as St. Edmund's, Riddlesdown and St. Antony's, Hamsey Green.

SOURCES

CORDEROY, M., & JONES, R. (Eds.) (1981) *Sanderstead Cricket Club Centenary 1881-1981*

Factfile, Townswomen's Guilds 1989

GARNER, GWEN (1995). *Extra Ordinary Women: a History of the Women's Institutes*, WI Books

GLYNNE-JONES, R. (1994) *Purley Downs Golf Club – A Centenary Celebration.* Purley Downs Golf Club

Local directories and organisations

Sanderstead Literary Society

Other local societies

A leisure centre in the future, now that we have acquired a pub?

Chapter 17

The Natural World Around Us

by Joy Gadsby

The natural history of Sanderstead is inextricably linked with the social history of the village, and reflects the human lifestyles and practices of the past and of the present. The natural world around us demonstrates the persistence, innovation and adaptability of nature, and also the losses, neglect and struggle for existence in the face of human indifference and lack of understanding of the environment. Happily attitudes are now changing as people become more aware of the fragility of the earth and its resources.

One of the most beautiful but totally unexpected sights in recent years occurred in 1990 when a great expanse of scarlet poppies sprang up in the fields flanking Mitchley Hill and Rectory Park. It was a sight that would have been very common in the 18th century in the days of Farmer Russell and indeed even as far back as the Iron-age 'Atwood' farmstead in the first century AD, but one lost in post-World War II years through excessive use of herbicides and pesticides. In 1996 the poppies were back, this time mingling spectacularly with the blue of flax.

There are many ways of studying the natural world, but three themes come to mind when considering the natural history of a suburban 'village' such as Sanderstead:

> the persistence and resilience of nature
>
> the appearance of the unexpected
>
> the opportunity to become a nature detective

THE PERSISTENCE AND RESILIENCE OF NATURE

It is fortunate that there is a substantial amount of open space within the parish boundaries, and over 50% of the land area is designated Metropolitan Green Belt. There are still agricultural fields, ancient woodland, 19th century plantations, ponds and chalk downland. There are also more 'tamed' open spaces, for example golf courses, the Gruffy, old quarries, recreation grounds, railway embankments, car parks and of course private gardens. All of these are important reservoirs of wild life and reflect not only the human practices and pastimes of today but also the lingering ghosts of former land use patterns.

Ancient Woodland

Woodlands can be described as 'primary', 'ancient semi-natural' or 'secondary'. Very little primary woodland exists in Britain today, that is, woodland that has remained in existence since the days of the primeval forests that once covered almost the whole of the land. Ancient semi-natural woodland has been managed over the centuries and has been in existence since before AD 1600. That too is rare in Britain as a whole but Sanderstead, and neighbouring Selsdon are endowed with many acres of it. Secondary woodland, dating from post 1600, is also to be found, for example, at Sanderstead Plantation and Purley Beeches.

Within the parish boundary the largest area of ancient woodland is King's Wood – about 147 acres today and almost the same size as it was 200 years ago, when it was described in Thomas Wigsell's will as '150 acres be it more or less'. The correct name for the woodland is Sanderstead Woods; it was certainly in existence at the time of Elizabeth I and may possibly be the same or part of the 'woodland at 30 pigs' mentioned in Domesday Book. The name King's Wood rightly belongs to a much smaller piece of woodland on the eastern side of Kingswood Lane, the name having been transferred in error when the first Ordnance Survey map was made early in the 19th century.

The sinuous boundary of King's Wood, which also forms the parish boundary. 1998

A Bourne Society group studies an interesting find in King's Wood. 1986

THE NATURAL WORLD AROUND US

King's Wood contains many of the features that identify it as ancient – It is on the parish boundary; it has sinuous boundaries, at least on the south and eastern sides where it is still marked by a bank and ditch; it contains old coppice stools, that is trees which have been cut down to the base many times and encouraged to grow 'multi-stems' to provide small, useful timber; it has a very rich flora, including species known to be associated with ancient woodland, e.g. Midland Hawthorn, Crab Apple, Wild Pear, Wild Cherry, Wood Anemone, Woodruff, Early Purple Orchid, Wood Sorrel, Dog Violet, Goldilocks (the woodland buttercup) and Wood Mellick. These species taken in isolation do not necessarily indicate an ancient site, but growing together in a rich community they are a strong indicator of it. More than 150 flowering species have so far been recorded there.

In late spring these woods are carpeted with bluebells, something we should not take for granted. In a European context the bluebell is a rare species, and it may now be threatened by global warming.

The age of the trees is not in itself a gauge of antiquity, although there are still a few large oaks, probably planted by Thomas Wigsell in the 18th century, which survived the great storm of October 1987. The woodland will have been replanted many times throughout its life-span and was a very important source of materials for the community. It produced timber for house building (perhaps used in the building of the parish church and 'The White House'), furniture, carts, wheels, barrels, hurdles, tools and domestic utensils of all kinds as well as fuel for the villagers. Oak bark was used in the tanning of leather; the inner bark of Lime trees was used to make twine or 'bast'; Elder had many uses and Birch bark, which is very flexible, could be used to make shoes. Acorns and other nuts and fruits provided food for domestic animals, especially pigs, and some of them for people too.

The local woods were converted into game coverts in the latter part of the 19th century, when locally produced timber became uneconomic against competition from imported sources and the increased use of coal for fuel.

Coombe Wood on the summit of Riddlesdown – A painting by Ethel Hall *c.*1900
Courtesy of Croydon Library

The history of King's Wood is repeated in Mitchley Wood and in the smaller 'shaws', such as Ansteys Berry Shaw which is partly ancient and partly recently colonised.

In more recent times, during World War II, the woods provided training grounds for the army and camouflage for antiaircraft guns. Traces of this occupancy can still be found.

Other extensive areas of ancient semi-natural woodland occur at Croham Hurst, Selsdon Wood, parts of Little Heath and at Farleigh. Thanks to their economic importance in the past and some energetic conservation lobbying in more recent times, these woods still give pleasure today and should be jealously guarded as part of our heritage.

Village Ponds

Ponds have been very important in the life and economy of any settlement or village from earliest times right up to the present century, and those remaining are still an important feature in the local landscape. Most ponds are man-made, either by lining a natural hollow with puddled clay or allowing the natural drainage to 'pond up' or the dew to collect instead of evaporating or by damming up a natural watercourse. There were once about 350,000 recorded ponds in England and Wales, but without regular management they silt up, become choked with water weeds and eventually develop into scrub and woodland – a process known as 'natural succession'.

In the past there would have been a number of ponds in Sanderstead. Today only two of these ponds remain (although many others have been created in gardens), the main one being by the Gruffy in the centre of the village and the other at Hamsey Green, on the corner of Limpsfield Road and Kingswood Way. At least one survived within living memory in King's Wood and there would have been others on the farms and downland.

Sanderstead Village Pond by the Gruffy

Besides being very valuable and necessary for a water supply, both for the villagers and for the numerous animals using the drove roads to and from market, ponds were also important in the local economy, as for example by providing reeds that could be used for thatching and rushes that could be strewn, plaited into mats or used for rushlights. Even the mud would have been valuable in the 'wattle and daub' construction of the earliest houses.

The vegetation of Sanderstead pond has almost certainly been influenced by the planting of some species in the past, but includes some attractive plants, including Yellow Iris, Fringed Waterlily, Water Crowfoot, Reedmace, and three species of Duckweed. The fauna includes Common and Crested Newts, Common Frog, Water Snails, Water Boatmen, Pond Skaters, Dragonflies and Damselflies, and many other invertebrates. In recent years a pair of Mallard and Moorhen have several times raised families, and in 1988 a Bastard Mallard, probably a cross between a Mallard and a Muscovy according to one authority, stayed for several weeks; its photograph made the local news.

The pond at Hamsey Green disappeared for many years, having silted up, but was restored in the 1970s. Most of the vegetation has been introduced, but some has become established naturally and it makes an attractive feature at the corner of Kingswood Way.

Chalk Downland

In the past the North Downs were important in the village economy. The thin soils over the chalk are warm and dry although only marginally suited for arable crops such as Oats and Barley. They yielded excellent herb-rich grazing for sheep – an important part of the farming scene locally until the early part of the 20th century. Within the parish lies part of Riddlesdown and also Sanderstead and Purley Downs, which were converted into Purley Downs Golf Course in 1894.

Continuous grazing kept the grass short and allowed a rich variety of wild flowers, adapted to the conditions, to flourish. With the cessation of sheep grazing, the rabbits continued the 'mowing' until the deliberate introduction of myxomatosis in 1953. The result of this disease was disastrous both for the rabbit population and the downland flora, as taller aggressive species and scrub took over. On the golf course, however, through sensitive management, many downland flowers survive, particularly in the roughs, including rarities such as Round-headed Rampion, Dropwort and Orchids.

In recent years the City of London has reintroduced sheep grazing on Riddlesdown as a conservation measure with considerable success. Cowslips have re-established themselves, and in summer we can once again enjoy Dropwort, Horseshoe Vetch, Scabious, Round-headed Rampion and many other species that would have been familiar to our shepherding ancestors. This in turn has enabled a rich invertebrate fauna to develop and in particular the many species of butterfly and moth now to be found there give delight to the eye in spring and summer.

All Saints' Churchyard

Few people would think of the churchyard as a wildlife haven, yet in the old churchyard there is between 8-10% of the British native flora represented, and a surprisingly rich fauna too. Managing a churchyard for the conservation of wildlife has to be a matter of compromise – a delicate balance between nature conservation, tidiness and sensitivity for those whose loved ones are buried there. In recent years there has been a strong movement nationwide towards conservation, through the 'Living Churchyard' project, and in Sanderstead the north side of the churchyard is now managed with wildlife very much in mind. The greatest treasure is the Meadow Saxifrage *Saxifraga granulata*; this was once a common plant of neutral grasslands but is now almost entirely confined to churchyards on sandy soils and is becoming quite rare. It is a delicate, attractive plant and Sanderstead churchyard boasts one of the best sites for it in Surrey.

Other species that reflect the meadowland origins out of which the churchyard was carved many centuries ago include Ladies' Bedstraw, Ladies' Smock, Bulbous Buttercup, Red Clover and Meadow Vetchling. Altogether

Meadow Saxifrage *(Saxifraga granulata)* – now abundant in the churchyard

over 150 flowering species have now been recorded in this one acre of land.

The churchyard extension at the top of Church Way is on rather different soil and has a different origin, having been part of Birtsclose Plantation until it was acquired by the church in 1936. It contains some very fine old trees, including Wild Cherry, Lime and Sweet Chestnut, and reflecting its woodland origins Bluebell, Wood Anemone and Wild Arum are to be found, as well as garden escapes such as the little blue *Anemone blanda*. So far 112 species of wild flowering plants have been recorded there.

Also important are the lichens. The proximity to busy main roads and the pollution generated by heavy traffic limits the number of species able to survive, because some lichens are extremely sensitive to atmospheric pollution. Nevertheless because of the many old gravestones, particularly those made of limestone, which provide good lichen habitats, 32 species have been recorded in All Saints' churchyard in recent years and of these five are seldom recorded in the south of England.

In the churchyard many invertebrate species occur, including the Yellow Meadow Ant, Common Field Grasshopper, the occasional Dragonfly, and at least 12 species of Butterfly – a creature which has long been regarded by Christians as a symbol of the resurrection and therefore very appropriate in a churchyard. Snails are plentiful, including the colourfully-banded White- and Dark-Lipped Hedge Snails. Frogs, Toads and Common Lizards find a home there too.

Mammals

Mammals are well represented in all the different habitats in Sanderstead. Foxes, rarely seen in the years before 1950, are now so common that scarcely a day passes without a sighting, be it in woodland, downland, churchyard or in gardens. Badger, Stoat, Weasel, Mole, Common Shrew, Grey Squirrel, Bank and Field Vole, Wood Mouse, Pipistrelle Bat, and in recent years Roe Deer, all enjoy the shelter of the woodlands. Most are nocturnal and therefore rarely seen but their signs and tracks are plainly visible to the observant visitor.

A Bank Vole's hole in the churchyard

THE NATURAL WORLD AROUND US

Birds

There are good opportunities for bird-watching in Sanderstead and the local branch of the Royal Society for the Protection of Birds is well supported. Some species have declined over the years, being less able to adapt to loss of habitat from housing development. Skylarks and Lapwings were once a common sight over the farmland, but today the Lapwing is no longer seen within the confines of the parish and the Skylark is rare, being seen only over Riddlesdown and occasionally over Purley Downs Golf Course. Rooks have declined since the great storm of 1987 when many of their roosting sites in the tops of tall trees were lost. Other species have increased; Jay and Siskin are much more common than they once were and the Collared Dove, now a common sight, has only been seen in Britain since about 1955 having spread across Europe from the east. Magpies and Crows have also increased in number.

Over 50 species have been recorded in local woodlands, including most members of the Tit family, Greater, Lesser Spotted and Green Woodpeckers, Cuckoo, Nuthatch, Tree Creeper, Chiff-chaff, Willow Warbler, Blackcap, Lesser Whitethroat, Tawny Owl as well as the commoner species that regularly visit local gardens. Herons raid the garden ponds, Kestrels hover overhead, and the Sparrowhawk has made a spectacular comeback in recent years.

Swallows, Swifts and House Martins all visit in summer, but in smaller numbers in recent years. Reasons for the decline are not fully understood, but possibly relate to the expansion of desert conditions in North Africa, which they have to cross on their spring and autumn migrations.

The importance of gardens particularly for birds cannot be over-stressed. Many species now depend for their survival on the 'service stations' provided with bird tables and regular all the year provision of suitable foods is an essential supplement to their food supply.

APPEARANCE OF THE UNEXPECTED

One never knows what may appear in a residential area, especially if it has a relatively recent rural past. Nature is incredibly persistent and adaptable. Some species suddenly appear having lain dormant for years, from an earlier use of the land. Who would expect, for example, to find Lucerne *Medicago sativa* in a station car park or Wild Strawberry along a busy main road, yet both have occurred. A large colony of Bee Orchids suddenly made an appearance in June 1995 in one of the local fields, where they had not been seen before in living memory. One of the bearded lichens, *Usnea subfloridana,* normally only found in very unpolluted areas was found on many of the Oaks which fell in King's Wood during the 1987 storm. Gardens on former farmland suddenly sprout wheat in the flower border, Scarlet Pimpernel among the runner beans and Field Madder on the lawn.

Foreign invaders have also occurred, perhaps travelling in tourist luggage, in trouser turn-ups or on aeroplane tyres; or introduced by birds or through the human agency of wild bird seed. The Flowering Nutmeg, *Leycesteria formosa,* a native of the Far East is to be found in Riddlesdown woodland, Japanese Knotweed, *Fallopia japonica,* in common wasteland, and the minute New Zealand Pygmyweed, *Crassula helmsii,* has recently arrived and is causing consternation among conservationists as it has invaded Sanderstead and other local ponds.

**Bee Orchids (*Ophrys apifera*)
suddenly appeared in a local field**

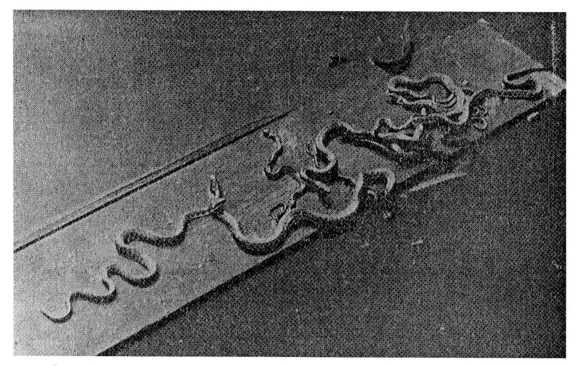

Over 200 snakes escaped the drought in a swimming pool at the back of an empty house in Purley Downs Road in 1975.   In all 43 Adders and 170 Grass Snakes were rescued by the RSPCA.   Another 47 Grass Snakes were found dead.   *Croydon Advertiser*

THE UNEXPECTED!

Have you lost anything?

Foxes have taken to 'borrowing' things and dumping them in other people's gardens. The residents' answer is the 'Fox Box'!

Some introductions from abroad have been more welcome. Probably the best kept secret in Sanderstead is the wide range of exotic trees to be found in the Wettern Tree Garden which includes many rare species.

OPPORTUNITY TO BE A NATURE DETECTIVE

The natural world can often provide a key to human history. The Lucerne that appeared in a car park, once one of Farmer Russell's fields, could have been carried recently by a bird but it is not a crop commonly grown today, whereas it was once a common component of crop rotation. Similarly Sainfoin occurs occasionally in the fields that were once part of Borough Farm. This was a nutrient-rich fodder crop much favoured for the finer breeds of horses, and it is probably no coincidence that Farmer William Wilson was well known nationally as a breeder of horses and as a judge at horse shows.

The pattern of former farmland can often be detected by surviving hedgerows. The greater the number of woody species in a hedge the older it is likely to be, although the age of a hedge cannot be assessed reliably simply by counting the species; the type of species is also important and corroboration from documentary or other evidence is needed for certainty. A short stretch of hedgerow alongside Sanderstead Hill contains 15 species of woody plants, and reference to old maps proves it to be part of a former field boundary of Briton Hill Farm which was sold for development in the 1930s. It may even have been the boundary of one of the old common fields, the North Field, and Saxon in origin. Similar hedges, with up to eight species, run along the bottom of the gardens in Kirkly Close, formerly belonging to Fox Farm and known in the 1930s as 'Morley's fields'. Another interesting hedgerow can be found at the junction of Village Way and Limpsfield Road, alongside what was formerly the farm track from Borough Farm to Mitchley.

Many old trees are to be found in Sanderstead, predating the properties in the grounds of which they now grow. The Beech tree outside Sanderstead library is estimated to be about 200 years old, whereas the library was built in 1937. Was the Cedar of Lebanon after which Cedar Court is named really planted, as tradition says, by Elizabeth I? It is quite likely that she did visit 'Sanderstead Court', the mansion on the site when

Young 'nature detectives' at work in Sanderstead Churchyard

A HISTORY OF SANDERSTEAD

John Ownstead was Lord of the Manor. However, Alan Mitchell, an authority on tree introductions, gives 1638 as the earliest date for the introduction of the Cedar of Lebanon, and therefore a later date is much more likely.

Yew trees have always been associated with longevity and there are many fine specimens in Sanderstead, not only in the churchyard. Were they planted for a specific reason? Did superstition play a part? Did they mark an ancient boundary or route?

There are two small copses surviving between the 5th, 6th and 7th fairways on Purley Downs Golf Course. They served as a marker for aircraft taking part in air races from Croydon Airport, and were retained on request.

A fox's earth that had existed for many years in a roadside bank survived the upheaval of a major road works which lasted for many months, and was back in use within three days of the reopening of the road. Some of the badger setts in local woodlands, with their labyrinths of tunnels, are almost certainly centuries old.

These are just some examples of the mysteries to be solved, local knowledge to be discovered, and enjoyment to be had from becoming a nature detective. Sanderstead, with its long, continuous history, is a very good place to start.

SOURCES

GREENOAK, F. (1985). *God's Acre.* Orbis Publishing

POLLARD, L., HOOPER, M.D. & N.W. MOORE. *Hedges.* New Naturalist Series. Collins

RACKHAM, O. (1988). *History of the Countryside*

Surrey Wildlife Trust - Flora and fauna records

Research by Gwyneth Fookes, Joy Gadsby & Jane McLauchlin.

Chapter 18

People Past and Present

by all contributors to the book

There have been many men and women who have made an impact in their time on life in Sanderstead but who have not so far figured in this history, or only briefly so. This chapter seeks to redress this omission by giving a brief glimpse into their lives and work. There are many who merit inclusion, but space is limited. The following have been selected from different walks of life to give insight into the development of the Sanderstead of today:

In Date Order -

QUEEN ETHELFLEDA was almost certainly a descendant of Aelderman Alfred, a member of Alfred the Great's court. He had left his land at Sanderstead to his wife and daughter and entailed it through the female line. Ethelfleda was the first wife of King Edgar, Alfred the Great's great-grandson, by whom she had a son, Edward. The marriage and the birth of Edward took place before Edgar became king, a point which was to be of significance later. Edgar acceded to the throne in AD 959 and by 965 had divorced Ethelfleda and married Aelfrith, by whom he had another son Aethelred (the Unready). Ethelfleda retired to the Convent of Wilton, where she became the Abbess, and it was probably then that she gave the Manor of Sanderstead to the Benedictine Monastery of Winchester in 964.

When Edgar died in 975 he was succeeded by his son Edward, but two and a half years later Edward was murdered and Aethelred acquired the throne – on the basis that he was born 'in the purple' when his father was already king.

Edward was at first buried without ceremony but later, following reports of miracles attributed to him, was given an honourable funeral at Shaftesbury and was canonised by the Roman church during Aethelred's reign. We do not know when Ethelfleda died or how much she knew of the fate or fame of her son, but it is to her that we owe the long association of Sanderstead with the Benedictine monks of Winchester which lasted until the Dissolution of the Monasteries in 1539 – a period of nearly 600 years.

LEWIS AUDLEY was born in 1618 into a family of some position but not great wealth. He at first intended to become an Anglican priest, and was ordained deacon at Peterborough in 1641, but then left the church to join Oliver Cromwell's new model army. He quickly rose to the rank of captain and was later promoted to major-general. On leaving the army he came to live at Purley Bury, having married a widow, Mary Hawtrey (née Bedell). Mary Audley has a fine marble tomb in All Saints' Church. Audley was made a commissioner for Surrey, and in 1657 was a member of the Commission of Enquiry into Ecclesiastical Matters and a Justice of the Peace. It is thought that it was due to his influence that Sanderstead was one of the few churches allowed to continue using the Anglican liturgy during the puritan regime of the Commonwealth. Several marriages were conducted at his house at Purley Bury. At the restoration of Charles II, he was pardoned and retired quietly to Cambridgeshire, where he died in 1670.

A Mellish coat of arms

HENRY MELLISH was a member of a large family, many of whom were Merchant taylors – they were prominent not only in south-east England but also in Nottinghamshire and Yorkshire. Henry is described in his memorial in All Saints' Church as being a Merchant of the Levant, a company set up in the reign of Elizabeth I to further trade between England, Turkey and the Middle East, particularly in fabrics, wool and carpets. Henry lived in Sanderstead but travelled for many years in foreign countries in pursuit of his trade, and sadly succumbed to an unknown lingering illness from which he died in 1667. His business interests were almost certainly based in and conducted from London, and he could perhaps be considered as one of Sanderstead's first commuters.

BENJAMIN BEESON was born in 1830 at King's Lynn, Norfolk, and at the age of 11 had the good fortune to be taken into the house of a gentleman of that county as a trainee groom. He learned good horsemanship and also to read and write, and at the age of 22 enlisted in the 11th Hussars. He was one of the few survivors of the ill-fated Charge of the Light Brigade at the Battle of Balaclava in 1854. On leaving the army in 1856, he joined the Metropolitan Police, in which he served for 26 years, much of that time in Sanderstead. His 'manor' included Whyteleafe, Warlingham, Chelsham and Kenley as well as Sanderstead, and he was a well-known figure in the area on his white horse, Sally. He died on Christmas Day 1908, and was given a hero's funeral at All Saints' Church.

The Sanderstead Mounted Patrol Station, probably as Benjamin Beeson would have known it. A drawing by Edwin Horne - 1933. *Courtesy of Croydon Library*

BISHOP ANTHONY THOROLD was born in 1825 and married twice. His first wife was Henrietta Green whom he married in 1850 and by whom he had three children, who died at the ages of 2, 10 and 21. Henrietta herself died in 1859, before the deaths of her second two children. Six years later, while a curate at Holy Trinity, Marylebone, Anthony Thorold married Emily Labouchiere, by whom he had three more children – a son, Algar Labouchiere Thorold, and two daughters, Dorothy and Sybil. Emily died in 1877, not long after Anthony had been appointed Bishop of Rochester. Note the meteoric rise from curate in 1865 to bishop in 1877 – in just 12 years. In 1877 the Bishop moved into 'Selsdon Park' (Sanderstead was then within the Diocese of Rochester) and lived there until he was translated to Winchester in 1890. Whilst at Selsdon Park he ordained 57 men to the priesthood in All Saints' Church and their names are recorded.

CHARLES PACE was born in 1844 'over stables in Oxford Street, London'. He was one of nine children and at the age of 10 started work at a greengrocer's for 4d. a day. After a while he hired a goat and cart from Westminster Bridge and took children for rides to Greenwich, making a very good profit. At the age of 14 he had saved enough money to set up in business delivering milk. For 3s. 8½d he purchased a milk can, measure, and 2½d worth of milk. He worked hard and at the age of 17 was able to marry, renting a house in Walworth for 9s. a week and letting out two of the rooms for 4s. 6d. By this time he was selling 20 quarts of milk a day. Eventually he bought 20 cows and 22 horses and vans. In the 1890s he came to Sanderstead, where he rented Purley Farm; by now he had a herd of 220 cows. He became the owner of 200 houses in the area, the largest grain and manure merchant in London, and the largest dairy farmer in Croydon, being connected with the Croydon cattle market for many years. He was also a Life Governor of Croydon General Hospital.

FRANCES DORA SMITH was the granddaughter of George Smith of Selsdon Park. In 1853 she married the 13th Earl of Strathmore and is thus the grandmother of Queen Elizabeth, the Queen Mother. To the Smith family we owe the church clock at All Saints', with its legend 'The hours perish and are laid to our account' *(Pereunt et imputantur)*, and the Queen Mother acknowledged the connection by giving very generously to the restoration of the clock after World War II. Many of the Smith family are buried in All Saints' churchyard, in the family vault, and there are memorials to several of them on the walls of the church, including Frances Dora and her father Oswald Smith.

Above left: Memorial to Henrietta Smith, who left 111 direct surviving descendents

Above right: Memorial to Oswald Smith, father of Frances Dora Smith

Left: The Smith family vault in All Saints' Churchyard

L. LAWRENCE was born in 1882 and died on 5th November 1967. He was known to his friends as 'Curly', but as 'LBSC' to steam locomotive model-makers, both in Great Britain and overseas, a pseudonym deriving from a period in his early years when he was a locomotive fireman with the London, Brighton and South Coast Railway. He wrote regularly in the magazine *The Model Engineer* for over 40 years, and had a genius for model steam locomotive design, publishing 112 designs and writing over 3000 articles in the course of 44 years. He also wrote *The Live Steam* book on model railway locomotives, which was published by Percival Marshall & Co. in 1950. In 1997 many of his models still feature in the catalogues of major firms world-wide and the house in which he lived near Purley Oaks station was notable for the presence of a railway semaphore signal in its garden, which appropriately backs onto the London to Brighton railway line.

TOM SHERLOCK was born in Holloway, North London, in 1885. The family had a business as suppliers of chemists' sundries under the style of Sherlock Brothers, with premises in City Road, near *The Angel* Islington. The business there still exists. The family came to Sanderstead in the 1890s. His mother died in 1910 and is buried in Sanderstead churchyard.

Tom Sherlock

In World War I Tom Sherlock served as a Captain in the Army, and in 1918 married Bertha. After the war he continued to do voluntary service in Egypt and the Middle East, and their eldest son was born there and is proud of the fact that he was baptised with water from the River Jordan. In 1921 he returned to England and worked in the family business, commuting daily. His heart was in Sanderstead, and he took great interest in its history and in local affairs. He was for several years President of the Sanderstead Preservation Society, and also captained the Sanderstead Cricket Club. He bought the ground adjoining the Sawmill, and the local cricket team still plays there. Bertha died tragically in a road accident. Later he married his cousin, Nan, who was a hospital matron. Both his wives and Tom himself are commemorated in All Saints' Church and Tom has a second memorial in the form of a fountain by Sanderstead Pond.

Malcolm G. Sharpe, Esq

MALCOLM SHARPE, an architect, came to the Croydon area in 1895 and lived for many years at the corner of Arkwright Road and Church Way, Sanderstead. He worked tirelessly for the conservation of the woodlands and open spaces in the Bourne Society's area and served on the committees that eventually secured Croham Hurst, Little Heath Woods, Purley Beeches and Selsdon Woods as public open spaces. He was honorary secretary of the Croydon & District Commons and Footpaths Preservation Society, and was later elected to the council of the National Trust. Those who were members of the Guide and Scout movements before and during World War II will have enjoyed many camp fires and weekend camps in Mr. Sharpe's field – a large open space at the back of his bungalow – and remember him as a very kind, self-effacing, but far-sighted benefactor. He died in 1948.

SIR ARCHIBALD PAGE was born in Alloa, Scotland, on 5th September 1875, the only son of a wool merchant. He studied both mechanical and electrical engineering and was amongst the first to realise the potential for electricity as a source of both power and light. He planned the first major municipal power station at Dalmarnoch, and in 1927, as general manager of the newly formed Central Electricity Board, directed the construction of the 'National Grid' and the standardisation of the frequency of the system. In 1943 he was awarded the Faraday Medal of the Institute of Electrical Engineers, a body on which he served as president. In semi-retirement he lived at 1 West Hill, Sanderstead, where he died on 7th March 1949.

COUNCILLOR FRANK MOIR for 33 years was a member of Coulsdon & Purley Urban District Council and served on various committees being appointed chairman in January 1938. He also played an active part in the Sanderstead Ratepayers' Association, later renamed the Sanderstead Residents' Association, working tirelessly for the good of the people of Sanderstead. He died on 21st October 1962, and following a local appeal a memorial rose garden was planted in the grounds of Sanderstead Library. Moir Close is also a reminder of him.

ERIC WETTERN was born in 1890 and was the youngest of three brothers. The family moved to Sanderstead in the early 1900s, living in Sanderstead Road. During World War I Eric served in the Royal Naval Division in Gallipoli, and later in France with the Royal Engineers. Meanwhile he had purchased a piece of land locally, and on leaving the army began developing it as a garden. The three brothers were in partnership in the firm of Wettern Brothers Ltd. which began as shipbrokers and importers and later expanded into builders' merchanting, pre-cast concrete manufacturing and sand quarrying. The head office moved from London to Croydon in 1940. Eric Wettern was a lifelong member of the Royal Horticultural Society, and his garden was his pride and joy. In it he planted many rare trees grown from seed which he collected during his business travels abroad. In 1965 he donated the garden to the Borough of Croydon as a public open space, which is enjoyed to this day.

GODFREY TALBOT, author, broadcaster and journalist, was born in October 1908 and still lives in Sanderstead. He was the senior news reporter and commentator on the staff of the BBC from 1946-1969, and the official BBC observer accredited to Buckingham Palace for many years. In his early years he worked as a journalist on the *Yorkshire Post* and the *Manchester City News*, joining the BBC in 1937. He served as a BBC war correspondent during World War II, was mentioned in despatches and awarded the OBE. He has accompanied many royal tours and written several books about the Royal Family, including a biography of Queen Elizabeth the Queen Mother in 1973, and *Forty Years the Queen* in 1992. *In Who's Who* he lists under recreation 'keeping quiet'!

THOMAS JORDAN was a rose expert and owned a nursery in Sanderstead for 34 years, where Jordan Close is now sited. He was born in Crowborough, Sussex of a gardening family and worked in nurseries in Kent, Sussex and Nottinghamshire, before starting his own business on a 2½ acre site in Briton Hill Road. He was a member of the Royal National Rose Society and was a judge at many horticultural shows throughout Surrey. He listed fishing, shooting and bridge amongst his hobbies. He died in about 1985.

JAMES RELF senior, born in 1886, was another prominent gardener in Sanderstead and began his career working for Mr. Horniman in Forest Hill. At the turn of the century he was able to rent a plot of land near the railway line in Purley Oaks Road, where his successors are still carrying on the family business. At some stage during the incumbency of the Revd. Walker (1920-35), local residents had been allowed and even encouraged to dump their rubbish on land that fell away sharply at the side of the rectory. James Relf was approached to fence it in and level the ground. This he did by laying railway lines across the land, loading little trucks, and tipping the rubbish down the hill. He was later able to purchase the land and establish his second nursery on it. Here it stood until the great storm of 1987 destroyed his greenhouses. James Relf celebrated his 90th birthday on 5th September 1976 and died a few years later.

BASIL HOWARD TRIPP, who died on 18th December 1981 at the age of 78, was a much-loved local figure. He began work as a reporter with the *Surrey Mirror* and then went into industrial journalism, becoming editor of a number of magazines and technical journals. During World War II he served with the fire service, and had a lifelong interest in military affairs, including helping with the local army cadets. He later became editorial adviser to the *Naval Review*. He wrote a short but factual history of Sanderstead, and was a founder member of the Roman Catholic Church of the Holy Family. His son, the Right Revd. Howard Tripp, is an auxiliary bishop of the Roman Catholic Diocese of Southwark, and a Bourne Society plaque on the Old Forge (now the church hall) commemorates the anniversary of the 1000th mass to be celebrated there, at which Bishop Tripp officiated.

Memorial to Betty Margaret Zeal in All Saints' Churchyard.

DR. BETTY MARGARET ZEAL trained as a doctor of medicine at a time when women doctors were very few; she was in fact one of the earliest in the country. She specialised in the care of children and practised in several hospitals including Great Ormond Street, where a bed is dedicated to her memory. In 1940 she volunteered to accompany a large party of evacuee children to Canada, and sailed from Liverpool in the SS *City of Benares*. Only a few days into that ill-fated voyage, on the 17th September, and immediately after the departure of the naval escort vessels, the ship was torpedoed and sunk by a German U-boat. Dr. Zeal was last seen in one of the lifeboats, and is believed to have given up her place to a child she saw struggling in the water. Sadly she never returned to marry her fiancé, also a doctor.

RUTH ELLIS was the wife of a local dentist who lived on the corner of Sanderstead Hill and Purley Downs Road. She will always be remembered as being the last women to be hanged for murder in Britain. She was convicted at the age of 28 for the murder of her lover, David Blakeley, and her execution took place in 1955. This shocked the nation and contributed to the call to end capital punishment, which was abolished ten years later. Her husband, George Ellis, committed suicide in 1958.

WILLIAM GODDARD will always be associated with the building of St. Edmund's Church, Riddlesdown, one of the daughter churches of the parish of Sanderstead, the foundation stone of which was laid on 25th September 1954. Although the church before and after it was built had the first call on his time and energy, he served the local community in many other ways. One of the founder members of the Riddlesdown Residents' Association and a member of its committee, he was amongst those who defended the remaining open land on the estate from further development. He was intensely interested in education, and was on the governing bodies of several local schools, including Riddlesdown High School and Gresham and Atwood Primary Schools. He was also noted for his ability as a comic actor. He was for many years a churchwarden and shortly before his death in 1970 was given the honorary title of Warden Emeritus. A small extension to St. Edmund's is called the 'William Goddard Room' in his memory.

Ruth Ellis, the last woman to be hanged for murder in Great Britain

Sanderstead Centenarians

Above left: Miss Phyllis Revell, born 1895.

Above right: George Gadsby, born 1898

Left: Mrs Martha Rosier, died 1984 aged 103½

Sanderstead must be a healthy place to live!

SOURCES

All Saints' Parish Records

Anglo Saxon Chronicle

Croydon Advertiser

Croydon Local Studies Library

MARTIN, J.P.S. (1997). 'Lewis Audley – a Biographical Sketch'. Bourne Society *Local History Records* **36**

Sanderstead Residents' Association

Selsdon Gazette

The Oxford Dictionary of Saints

Who's Who and *Who was Who?*

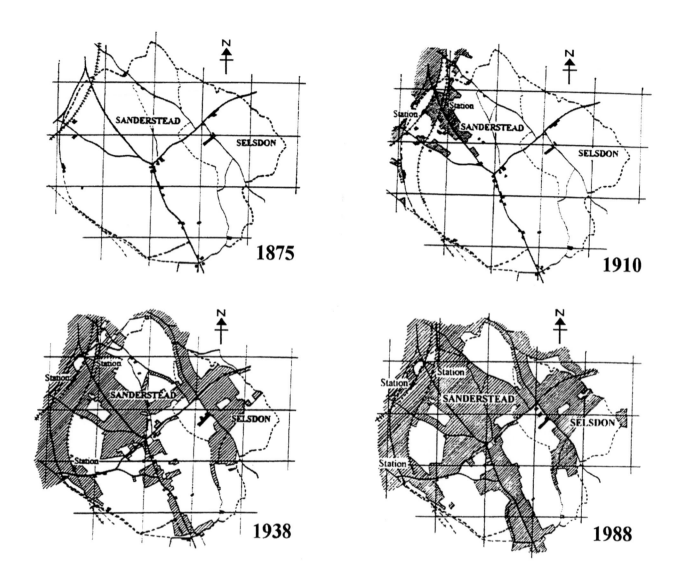

The Growth of Sanderstead in over a century –
1875 - 1988

Chapter 19

A to Z of Road Names

Researched by Vernon Briggs

Addington Road	An ancient trackway from the pond to Addington; it joins the Roman Road at Kent Gate.
All Saints' Drive	Modern road named after the parish church. It was built on ground belonging to 'The White House'.

Addington Road, Sanderstead *c.* 1935

Ansley Close	*See* Cherry Tree Green; part of the same estate.
Arkwright Road	Continuation of Church Way, the old bridleway to Croham Hurst. Esme Arkwright was a member of the Atwood family and was the last Lord of the Manor before it was sold in 1919.
Arundel Avenue	Named after the Duke of Norfolk's association with Arundel.
Ashdown Gardens	Associated with ash trees in the nearby woodland.
Atwood Close	Named after the Atwood Family, Lords of the Manor for centuries.

Audley Drive	After Lewis Audley, one of Cromwell's major-generals and local JP.
Balfont Close	An old field name on Borough Farm.
Barn Crescent	On the site of a barn.
Barnfield Road	After an ancient field name.
Barrowsfield	The name probably derives from a clump of trees – not to be confused with ancient burial mounds.
Beech Avenue	After Purley Beeches, which it borders.

Beech Avenue – from an old postcard. St. Anne's College in the background

Beechwood Road	Named after local woodland.
Blacksmith's Hill	Originally the track from the forge.
Blenheim Gardens	Associated with the battle fought by John Churchill, first Duke of Marlborough, in 1704.
Borrowdale Close	A local field name. At the Mitchley Hill end of Borrowdale Drive.
Borrowdale Drive	The road that was never completed. Look across the fields at the end and trace the intended course by the elevated manhole covers.
Brambledown Road	Part of the Fox Farm estate.
Brancaster Lane	Was a farm track and still undeveloped in 1929.
Brian Avenue	*See* Montague Avenue - the name of Mr. Thomas' son.
Briar Grove	A tangled plot before the road was built?

Brambledown Road, Sanderstead.

Briton Close	An old field name.
Briton Crescent	-do-
Briton Hill Road	An old farm track to Briton Hill Farm (See Sanderstead Hill)
Broadway Close	Built on Hamsey Green Farm land.
Broomhill Road	
Buttermere Gardens	Part of the Laing estate – the family had connections with the Lake District.
Cherry Tree Green	Cherry Tree Farm, a smallholding, until developed for housing in 1937.
Church Way	An ancient bridleway leading from the parish church to Croham Hurst.
Claremont Close	Built on Hamsey Green Farm land.
Clyde Avenue	On Hamsey Green Farm land.
Coombe Wood Hill	After the wood of that name.
Copperfield Close	
Copthorne Rise	An ancient name for one of the local farm houses or 'halls'.
Court Hill	The name of D. Montague Thomas's (the developer) house in Chipstead.
Courtlands Close	
Cranleigh Close	*See* Onslow Gardens – Viscount Cranleigh, another title of the Onslow Family.
Cranleigh Gardens	-do-

Dalegarth Gardens

Dalton Close Named after Atwood Dalton Wigsell.

Days Acre Old field name.

Derrick Avenue One of a group of names from the builder's family.

Derwent Drive *See* Buttermere Gardens – part of the Laing Estate.

Downsway From Sanderstead Downs.

Dunmail Avenue A road that was never built – services and drains are laid, but development was stopped by the Green Belt legislation.

East Hill *see* West Hill.

Edgar Road One of a group of names from the builder's family.

Ellenbridge Way John Ellenbridge was seized of the manor Croham when he died 1478.

Ellesmere Drive Built on Hamsey Green Farm land.

Elmfield Way Reflecting the original land-use.

Eskdale Gardens Part of the Laing estate – the family had connections with the Lake District.

Essenden Road Part of the Fox Farm estate.

Ewhurst Avenue Originally part of the Church Way footpath. Developed in the 1950s by A.J. Wait of Guildford, owner of Crystal Palace Football Club. His players were employed on the building site during the closed season.

Farm Fields Part of Briton Hill Farm land.

Field Close Part of the Cherry Tree Farm estate .

Florence Road One of a group of names from the builder's family.

Right: A house with family group, Florence Road. *c.*1908

Opposite: Florence Road today (1998)

Below: Glebe Hyrst – built in 1936 on land originally 'The Parson's Glebe'.

Gainsborough Drive

Glebe Close   On land belonging to the parish priest until the 19th century.

Glebe Hyrst   -do-

Limpsfield Road *c.* 1924. Beechview Cottages (18th century) in the foreground

Glebe Way	-do-
Glossop Road	
Gordon Avenue	From the builder's family.
Grisedale Close	Part of the Laing estate.
Grisedale Gardens	-do-
Hamsey Way	On Hamsey Green Farm land.
Harbledown Road	
Harewood Gardens	From the King's Wood game reserve which it borders.
Hazelwood Grove	On the site of hazel woodland.
Heathurst Road	
Hill Barn	Named after a house originally on the site.
Hills Mead Way	
Hilton Way	On Hamsey Green Farm land. Named by the estate surveyor in 1952.
Holmwood Avenue	
Honister Heights	Part of the Laing estate.
Hook Hill	An ancient field name for the spur of land owned by Richard atte Hook in the middle ages.
Hurnford Close	On the site of a house of that name.
Hyde Road	After the Abbey of Hyde, to which Sanderstead once belonged.
Ingleborough Drive	Part of the Laing estate.

A TO Z OF ROAD NAMES

Jordan Close	After Mr. Jordan, a local rose grower.
Kendall Avenue	The builder's surname (see also Penwortham Road).
Kendall Avenue South	-do-
Kings Walk	Part of the Cherry Tree Farm estate.
Kingswood Avenue	After King's Wood, the local woodland.
Kingswood Lane	-do-
Kirkly Close	
Langley Oaks Avenue	On the site of an area of woodland.
Leighton Gardens	Built on Hamsey Green Farm land.
Lexington Court	Commemorates John Horne Tooke, another resident of 'Purley Bury House', supporter of American Independence (Treaty of Lexington).
Lime Meadow Avenue	After 'Lime Place', later called 'Place House', owned by Robert Mellish who died there in 1627.
Limpsfield Road	A prehistoric trackway to Limpsfield.
Love Lane	Disappeared at the turn of the century, but marked on the field map of 1844. Now the access road to the house called the Old Sawmill opposite the pond.
Lower Barn Road	From a field name.
Marshalls Close	Named after a local councillor.
Mayfield Road	Reflecting its rural origins.
Maywater Close	Named after a councillor.
Mitchley Avenue	Linked with Mitchley Wood.
Mitchley Grove	-do-
Mitchley Hill	-do-

Mitchley Hill, 1998

A HISTORY OF SANDERSTEAD

Moir Close	Built in 1956 and named after Councillor Frank Moir.
Montague Avenue	Named after the developer, D. Montague Thomas.
Montana Close	From a house of that name which belonged to the Wettern family.
Morley Road	After Morley, the last occupier of Fox Farm. No. 6 has the portal from the old rectory.
Norfolk Avenue	Named after the Duke of Norfolk.
Norman Avenue	One of a group of names from the builder's family.
North Down	On the Downs facing north.
Oak Apple Close	Part of the Cherry Tree Farm estate.
Onslow Gardens	Onslow was an important family in political circles. The Earls of Onslow have been Lord Lieutenants of Surrey at various times. Their seat is Clandon Park.
Orchard Road	Part of the Cherry Tree Farm estate – probably there was an orchard here.
Ownstead Gardens	After John Ownstead, keeper of the Queen's carriage for Elizabeth I and Lord of the Manor.
Parr's Close	Fulk Parr was tenant of Croham Manor in 1648.
Pear Tree Close	Was there a pear tree on this site? Part of the Cherry Tree Farm estate.
Penwortham Road	The builder, Joseph Kendall's home town in Cumbria.
Prince's Avenue	On Hamsey Green Farm land.
Prince's Close	-do-
Purley Bury Avenue	Named after 'Purley Bury House', once the home of the Atwood Family and at one time Lewis Audley.
Purley Bury Close	-do-
Purley Downs Road	On the line of an ancient lane across Purley Downs.

Purley Downs Road with the Lodge to Purley Bury House in the foreground. From an old postcard.

A TO Z OF ROAD NAMES

Purley Oaks Road — Created in 1903. Named after a clump of ancient oak trees.

Rectory Park — The old rectory once stood at the corner of this road.

Reddington Close

Riddlesdown Avenue — Named after Riddlesdown, sometime called Riddleysdown.

Riddlesdown Road — Part of the Roman Road from London to Brighton (Portslade).

Riddlesdown Road, where it opens out onto the Corporation of London's Riddlesdown

Ridge Langley — An old field name.

Riding Hill — -do-

Rydal Close — In the Lake District group of roads.

St. Mary's Road — After St. Mary's Church. Unique in Sanderstead – no postman ever delivers in this road!

Sanderstead Court Ave — Originally the drive to the Manor House.

Sanderstead Hill — Until 1936 known as Briton Hill – possibly an ancient Celtic trackway?

Sanderstead Road — Continuous with Sanderstead Hill.

Sandhurst Close — Reflecting the sandy nature of the local soil.

Sandhurst Way — -do-

Shaw Close — Shaw is a local name for a narrow wood planted as a wind break.

Shaw Crescent — -do-

A HISTORY OF SANDERSTEAD

Southcote Road   King Henry IV granted the manor of Croham jointly to William Oliver and John Southcote for an annual rent of 50 shillings.

Stanley Gardens   Commemorates the innovator and scientist of the Victorian era.

Station Approach   To the station!

Stockhams Close   An old field name.

Sundown Avenue   It faces the sunset at its junction with Sanderstead Hill.

Tandridge Gardens   After its neighbouring borough or hundred of Tandridge.

The Ridge Way   Marks the land boundary of Eli Davy's Trust (Whitgift Foundation) and Fox Farm.

The Windings   It does! The shape is probably determined by an old field boundary. It was once part of the medieval North Field.

The Woodlands   Once part of Sanderstead Plantation.

Theresa's Walk   On the site of St. Anne's College, probably after St. Theresa.

Timberling Gardens   Old field name.

Tindale Close

Trinity Close   Almost certainly relating to the Whitgift land ownership in the area.

Tudor Close   Built on Hamsey Green Farm land.

Victoria Avenue   One of a group of names from the builder's family.

Village Way   Originally the track from Borough Farm to Riddlesdown.

Wentworth Way   On land that was once Hamsey Green Farm and follows a field boundary.

West Hill   Both East Hill and West Hill were originally called Sanderstead Hill. West Hill was built on the line of the old Fox Farm footpath running from Sanderstead Road to Upper Selsdon Road.

Westfield Avenue   On the site of one of the three open fields in medieval times.

Wettern Close   Named after Eric Wettern who gave the Wettern Tree Gardens as a public open space.

Weybourne Close   The builders were Wey and Close!

Whimbrel Close   A species of small curlew.

White Hill Close   An old field name.

Wisborough Road

Woodview Close   It has a view of the wood! Part of the Cherry Tree Farm estate.

Yew Tree Walk   Follows the tree-lined carriage drive to Purley Bury House. The gatekeeper's lodge is on the corner

SOURCES

NEWBERRY, K. Bourne Society *Local History Records*

Tithe Apportionment Map

Chapter 20

A History of Selsdon

by Ted Frith

Except for an 80 year period in modern times, when it was closely linked with Sanderstead, Selsdon has always been part of Croydon. Selsdon was a detached portion of the parish of Croydon, and its medieval boundaries have remained virtually unaltered. In 1883, when Croydon became a Borough, it was legally compelled to discard its detached part, and Selsdon was attached to the parish of Sanderstead. In 1884 it became part of the Croydon Rural District Council and in 1915 came under the new Coulsdon & Purley Urban District Council, but Selsdon returned to Croydon when the new London Borough was formed in 1965.

Selsdon is 360 hectares (889 acres) in area and lies physically on the north slopes of the North Downs and ranges from 90 metres to 165 metres above sea level. It is mostly on chalk subsoil – some clay with flints in the southern part. Selsdon is cut by two dry valleys running parallel east to west and there is now no surface water. There are two areas of high ground – the eastward continuation of the Sanderstead ridge – as far as the Selsdon Park Hotel, and three small hills of Thanet sands, capped with pebble beds in the area of Littleheath Woods. Selsdon was intersected by two thoroughfares, an ancient one along Selsdon Road running straight over where the hotel is now southwards towards Farleigh, with a track going off to Hamsey Green, and a lane westwards from Addington to Sanderstead.

Selsdon (the name means Seli's hill) is first mentioned in the will of the Kentish Ealderman Alfred *c.*871, when he left land in Sanderstead and Selsdon to his wife Waerburh. We do not know when Selsdon became incorporated within the Archbishop of Canterbury's lands in Croydon, but in a surviving report of 1193 from the Reeve to his Lordship, there is reference to the rent of a piece of land, Wodemannesrod, which is later shown as being in Selsdon. A taxation return for Surrey of 1332 lists 12 landholders for the Villata de Selesden, including Reginald Aleyn, William Joy, William the clerk and Isabel de Ouenstede, and the total tax for Selsdon was 17s.3d compared with 53s.9d for Sanderstead.

In 1492 Archbishop Morton ordered a terrier or survey of all his lands in Croydon and the document, which still survives, lists each field, the area of each strip, its tenant and the rental. From this it has been possible to determine the names of the fields and the tenants of Selsdon. There were still some large common fields – Northefeld, Estefield and Westfield – but in some cases only half the field was in strip cultivation, and even these were divided amongst two or three tenants. The chief tenant was Jeffery Ownstead (435 acres), and his kinsman, Robert, held 80 acres. Other fields mentioned are the Joigley Land Filde, Gosty Croft, Newlands and Kynges Wood (not the wood we know by that name now). No map was made, and it is difficult to say where some of the fields were. In a later survey, in 1543, there is reference to The Wygh (later Gee Wood) and it is suggested that this was an Old English word for a heathen shrine.

Also surviving is the Homage Jury for the Manor of Croydon from 1582 to 1834. This recorded all the changes of tenure (or copyhold), which had to be endorsed at the annual court of the manor, when a fee had to be paid – one heriot or the best beast, later transmuted to 3s.6d. The ownership of Selsdon was divided between the north, around the original Selsdon Farm (now the site of the hotel) and the south, then known as Allards.

The ownership of both farms can be traced until the end of the 18th century. Henry Ownstead (a relation of John Ownstead who owned Sanderstead manor) held Selsdon Farm in 1584. His successors, each of whom was a Henry, owned the farm until the Commonwealth, when Henry Bowyer became the tenant in 1660, and when Christopher Bowyer became the owner he rebuilt the farmhouse.

43

Item ... wedden ... ... — ijs

Item Jefferye Ovnsted ... — iijs

Item ... Morley ... ... — js

Addnsted

Item Jeffery Ovnsted ... — js

Item wedden ... — ijs

Item Jeffery Ovnsted ... — ...

Northfild

Item in primo Robert Ovnsted — ij ... — iijs

Item mr Ellmytrige ... — ij ... — iijs

Item Robert Ovnsted ... — iij yardes — js ob

Item Jeffery Ovnsted ... — iij ... — ...

Item Robert Ovnsted ... — iij ... — js

Item wedden ... — j ... — ijs

Item Robert Ovnsted ... — j ... — ijs

Item Jeffery Ovnsted ... — j ... — iijs

Item Tho. wedden ... — j yard — js

Item Robert Ovnsted ... — j ... — iiijs

Item Jeffery Ovnsted ... — iij ... — iijs

Item mr Morley ... — ...

Item Robert Ovnsted ... — ij ... — iiijs

Item mr Morley ... — ... — js

Item Jeffery Ovnsted ... — ... — ijs

Item mr Morley ... — ... — js

Item Robert Ovnsted ... — ij ... — iiijs

Item Jeffery Ovnsted ... — xviij ... — xijs iiijs

The tovne landfild

Item Jefferye Ovnsted ... in ... closes contaynyng ... — ...

Item Jeffery Ovnsted ... — ...

Item Tho. wedden ... — ij ... — iiijs

Extract from Archbishop Morton's Terrier of Croydon 1492

Villa de Sellistdowne

The previous page starts the Selsdon entry with Hereland and the last three entries for that field start this page.

	Item	Thos Wodden	1	acre	2d
		Jeffrey Ownstede	2	acres	4d
		Mr Morley	½	acre	1d
Ardonshel	Item	Jeffrey Ownstede	½	acre	1d
		Wodden next	3	acres	12d
		Jeffrey Ownstede	7	acres	2s 4d
Northefild	Item in primis	Robert Ownstede	2	acres	4d
		Mr Ellingbridge next	2	acres	4d
		Robert Ownstede next	3	yards	1½d
		Jeffrey Ownstede next	3	acres	12d
		Robert Ownstede next	3½	acres	10d
		Wodden next	1	acre	2d
		Robert Ownstede next	1½	acres	6d
		Jeffrey Ownstede next	1½	acres	6d
		Thos Wodden next	1	yard	1d
		Robert Ownstede next	1	acre	4d
		Jeffrey Ownstede next	3	acres	3d
		Mr Morley next	½	acre	1d
		Robert Ownstede next	2	acres	8d
		Mr Morley next	½	acre	1d
		Jeffrey Ownstede next	½	acre	2d
		Mr Morley next	½	acre	1d
		Robert Ownstede next	2	acres	8d
		Jeffrey Ownstede next	38	acres	12s 8d
The Joigly Landfild	Item	Jeffrey Ownstede in dyvers closes containing	46	acres	10s 4d
		Jeffrey Ownstede next there	5	acres	10d
	Item	Thos Wodden next	2	acres	4d

The entries for this field continue on to the next page. The Terrier is held in Croydon Local Studies Library and this entry, based on Clarence Paget's transcription of the document, is reproduced by kind permission.

The fields described above relate to the area on the north side of present day Selsdon-Littleheath Woods and the area around Littleheath, Farley and Foxearth Roads.

Kingswood Lodge, the oldest building in Selsdon, undergoing restoration in 1998

Selsdon Park, a painting by J. Hassell, 1820.
Courtesy of Croydon Local Studies Library

Old Farleigh Road looking north-west from entrance to Selsdon Woods. *c.*1905

**Addington Road
Cottages**
***c.*1906**

***Courtesy of Croydon
Local Studies Library***

His son Henry died aged 90 in 1752; the farm passed to his wife, Ann, who remarried, and when she died, to her daughter, Ann, wife of Thomas Lane. The tenure of the southern part changed hands more frequently, but in 1708 Thomas Jewdry built a new house, which later was called 'Kingswood Lodge', and is the oldest house in Selsdon. In the earlier days misdemeanours were also dealt with at the court, and in 1636 Robert Lucas was fined 12d for surcharging the lord's common with his sheep, herding them with a shepherd contrary to the custom of the manor.

The first detailed map of Selsdon was published in 1800 in connection with the Croydon Enclosure award. The only buildings were the Selsdon Farm buildings and 'Kingswood Lodge'. The fields, all named (such as Hither, Middle and Further Fox Shot Hill), are now more familiar.

Exactly when Selsdon Farm was gentrified into Selsdon Park is not clear. Some work had been done around 1780, but *c.*1809 a local entrepreneur, William Coles, purchased the farm and began turning it into a mansion. He became bankrupt, and the property was purchased – possibly in 1810 – by George Smith, a banker and director of the East India Company. He completed its transformation into a mansion, landscaped the park and moved the road to Farleigh eastwards to its present position. George Smith erected a home farm and buildings, two lodges, and a new farm, together with a number of cottages along the southern side of Addington road. This farm was let to a tenant, and two of the cottages, built about 1815, still remain. In the 1830s Elizabeth Coppin kept one cottage as a beerhouse, one was always let to a policeman, and two labourers lived in their cottages for over 40 years.

George Smith was succeeded by his son, George Robert, and he in turn by his son, Ernald, who died aged 33, in 1872. The estate devolved upon his infant daughter, Mabel, but until she inherited, the mansion was let to the Bishop of Rochester. Her Coming of Age was celebrated in Selsdon on 30th July 1888, in pouring rain, and the following week she married the Hon. Alwynne Greville. George Smith also bought 'Kingswood Lodge', but it appears to have been frequently let, although the youngest of his sons, Alfred, lived there from 1869 until his death in 1886. In 1890 Mabel Greville decided to sell the whole estate, except Kingswood Lodge, which she owned until 1921. The Mansion and the land south of Addington Road was bought by a London printer, William Stevens, and the land to the north was bought by Charles Goschen and incorporated into the Heathfield Estate. Stevens died in 1900, and Selsdon Park was purchased by a Bermondsey brewer, Wickham Noakes, who used to celebrate his birthday each year with a large shooting party in Selsdon Woods.

Just after World War I, Selsdon – with its large house, two farms and about 20 cottages and a population of around 70 – was still very isolated, being only accessible by narrow lanes, although it was only three miles from Croydon. On 6th September 1923 Wickham Noakes died aged 80, his four sons having predeceased him, and on 25th January 1924 Harold Houlder, the then owner of 'Heathfield' was declared bankrupt. The country backwater of Selsdon was thus ripe for development. Noakes' property was sold very quickly; Selsdon Park was purchased by Allan Doble Sanderson, a London businessman and well known racing driver. He turned the mansion into a 23-bedroomed hotel. The land east of Old Farleigh Road was bought by Mr. Cresswell for £10,000 – no doubt with an eye for future development, and the Kingswood Way portion was divided into building plots by Percy Harvey Estates.

The 'Heathfield' lands north of Addington Road were bought by the Walton Heath Land Company, owned by the Liverpool builder William Costain. His firm had come south after World War I, and had built a prestigious estate at Kingswood north of Reigate. Encouraged by a government scheme whereby builders of housing for the lower income groups were given a subsidy for each dwelling, it is said that Costain was playing golf at Croham Hurst when his partner told him the land nearby was up for sale. Selsdon Garden Village, as it was called, and before the last war substantially a Costain development, started in September 1925 when the first houses were completed around the corner of Upper Selsdon and Addington Roads.

Costain built four estates in Selsdon. The first, between 1925 and 1931, began on the greenfield site extending towards Littleheath Woods, and Croham Valley Road, where new houses were also being erected. This entailed the construction of a new road, Farley Road, which was opened in style by Lord Clwyd and the local MP on 24th July 1926. In October 1931 Costain started the Croham Heights estate in Arundel Road and Norfolk Road. After Addington Road had been widened Costain erected a number of more contemporarily designed houses on the northern side in 1933, and in the following year commenced the final development in Selsdon, the Old Farleigh Road estate, comprising Benhurst Gardens and the neighbouring roads.

The only other major development was the Selsdon Park Estate of New Elvet houses to the south of Addington Road – around Abbey Road – started in 1930, but there was a pause in its completion when the original builders failed. Small builders were involved in Sylvan Close, Dulverton Road, and the last development in pre-war Selsdon, Ingham Road in 1939. Most of the houses in Old Farleigh Road and on the south side of Addington Road were built by individual builders. Selsdon's first council houses were built for £9010 by a Grimsby firm, Thompson & Sons, in Hawthorn Crescent in 1929, the land being purchased at the same time as the recreation ground. Even then the planning controls of the UDC prevented Kingswood Way from becoming a plotlands development; one man had his bungalow pulled down and in 1926 the plans for a bungalow for a Mrs M Thatcher were thrown out!

The impetus for a new Anglican church came from St.Peter's in South Croydon, in which parish Selsdon then was. Although the original site was to have been where the Baptist church is now, the current site became available. A mission hall was dedicated on 14th March 1927 ,and soon church organisations, such as the Scouts and Brownies were flourishing. Funds were raised for a permanent church, and the present St John the Divine building was consecrated by the Archbishop of Canterbury on 17th October 1936 – in the middle of the Abdication crisis. Nonconformists first met in Mr. Nichols' house in Byron Road, and after discussion it was decided to establish a Baptist church, which was opened in September 1927. It is believed that a chapel was in use at St. Columba's Roman Catholic church in Queenhill Road by the end of 1926, as a daughter church to St. Gertrude's in South Croydon.

Many of the first houseowners in the new Garden Village were married couples with children, and as the nearest school was in Sanderstead, the children had to walk there and back without the benefit of car or bus. Surrey County Council had foreseen the need for a school, and had acquired a site in Addington Road in 1926. In September 1927 a Government Inspector of Schools reported that there was no immediate need for a school, and the County Council decided not to proceed. The local MP was tackled at a meeting of the Residents' Association. Sanderstead was a mile away along a narrow road with heavy traffic; of 68 children on the books of the Sanderstead school, 51 came from Selsdon, so a new school was imperative. Fortunately the MP was persuaded to talk to the Duchess of Atholl, the Parliamentary Under-Secretary for Education. A temporary school of light construction for 164 children was opened in May 1928, and a permanent infants and junior (384 pupils) and central school for 240 was opened on 31st May 1931. However, no Grammar school facilities were provided before or even after the war, and Selsdon children had to travel to Purley or Coulsdon – there being no school bus, no direct bus to Purley, and no assistance with fares. Little Heath School was a small private school that opened in 1927.

When Costain first developed Selsdon it set aside an area off Queenhill Road as a miniature golf course. Over many years there have been calls in Selsdon for a swimming pool, yet when in 1933 Costain proposed to build a lido on the site, with swimming pool and cafe, the residents objected strongly. Earlier in 1928, proposals to erect a greyhound racing stadium where Abbey Road now is, were also turned down.

The first residents were very isolated, few had cars and the roads were too narrow for buses. Most of the men worked in Croydon or London and during the winter of 1925/6 they had no option but to walk down to South Croydon in the mornings and, of course, to walk back up in the evenings. In July 1926 Costain hired a small single-deck bus which ran up Upper Selsdon Road from South Croydon station. It was not until November that

East Surrey introduced its single-deck 417, soon replaced by a double-decker, which in turn became the 54 under London Transport. This was the only bus service to Selsdon for a number of years. In May 1929 Costain arranged for Tilling to operate another private bus from South Croydon up the unasphalted Farley Road as far as Brent Road, until London General introduced its 254 in December 1931. This service was not extended to Selsdon until March 1933; later it was re-routed to West Croydon as the 64, and extended to Addington in March 1936. From October 1930 until the outbreak of war Green Line buses ran up Upper Selsdon Road to Sanderstead, but despite Selsdon's link with Purley there was no direct bus service until late 1949.

Costain's bus c.1929 *Courtesy of Mrs Louise Bartlett*

It took over ten years for the Selsdon Wood Nature Reserve to be purchased. A small group of conservationists had bought 16 acres of Court Wood in 1925, and after years of public appeals (including a delightful Selsdon Wood Calendar produced in 1935 to raise funds) and consultations with and contributions from local authorities, the woods were formally opened by the Lord Mayor of London on 5th June 1936. Ownership was vested in the National Trust, but the Wood is administered by Croydon Council. Earlier the Residents' Association had pressed for retaining the Littleheath Woods in their natural state; indeed Costain's original plan had shown a road, The Woodlands, running parallel to Littleheath Road. The woods were saved, being opened on 24th May 1934, the cost of purchase being shared between the two local councils and public subscription.

The Selsdon Residents' Association was formed on 2nd January 1926, when 50 residents walked up to the Brand Hall in Sanderstead. In the years leading up to and immediately after the war, the association played a very important part in the development of the suburb. Its first success was in obtaining a reduction in the rateable value of the new houses, and constantly it badgered the local authority on all the problems of a new estate – road safety, frequency of bus services, street lighting, making up the new roads, nuisance from wireless loudspeakers and so on. It also encouraged social activities, and both the local cricket and tennis clubs owe their origins to the association. During the winter whist drives and later when the Garage Hall was opened, dances were organised and a small lending library was established in Costain's estate office. A Child Welfare centre was opened in the Baptist Hall in 1928 and the association sponsored the formation of a nursing association, employing its own district nurse.

As the 1930s progressed, Addington Road was widened and traffic became more of a problem. An unrealistic suggestion to impose a 10 mph speed limit by the school was not pursued, but there were several serious accidents by the entrance to the hotel. In 1935, just before the general election, a young Selsdon man, Paul Winterton, who was the Labour candidate for Mitcham, was involved in an accident at the Farley Road/Queenhill Road junction – his wife was seriously injured and later died on the eve of polling day.

Arctic conditions hit Selsdon at the end of 1927, with snow up to bedroom window level in Queenhill Road, and Upper Selsdon Road was closed to traffic for nearly a week. Selsdon was cold in the winter – witness the bus conductors' shouts of 'Siberia' or 'No Man's Land'! Although it claimed to be above the fog line, on a misty September morning in 1932, a French freight plane, en route for Croydon, crashed into trees at the side of the hotel, killing the pilot.

Selsdon Park Hotel was opened on 1st July 1926 at terms, inclusive of full *en pension*, for two persons from eight guineas. Tennis, croquet, billiards, dancing and the wireless were advertised, and for non-residents luncheon was 4s.0d and dinner 6s.6d. In 1929 J.H. Taylor laid out the golf course and later Sanderson purchased both 'Sanderstead Court' and 'Wickham Court', both converted into hotels. Selsdon Park Hotel was considerably enlarged in the years leading up to the war.

Selsdon enjoyed an active social calendar during the pre-war years – there were shows by the Horticultural Society, to whom Mr C.H.Middleton, the Radio Gardener, often spoke. The Selsdon Players gave dramatic performances, Scout and Guide groups were started, a British Legion branch was formed in 1932, and after the UDC had decided to accept responsibility for libraries, a branch library was opened in Langley Oaks in May 1936.

In 1932 a Selsdon Unemployment and Distress Committee was formed to organise work – such as the construction of paths in the newly opened Littleheath Woods – for local men out of work. The Labour and Conservative associations flourished. Rain rather spoilt Selsdon's celebrations of the Coronation, and for part of the afternoon the programme was switched to the Church Hall for community singing and the King's Broadcast. Although first mooted in 1931, it was not until 1939 that Selsdon built its underground public convenience. Planning permission for a public house in Selsdon was granted in 1938, but because of objections by the Baptist Church and local temperance groups it was not until 1956 that *The Good Neighbour* (now *The Stag*) was opened.

An appeal for volunteers for the Auxiliary Fire Service at the monthly residents' meeting in March 1938 was the first indication of the coming world conflict. In May the newly-appointed Air Raids Precautions Officer assured residents that Selsdon would be fortunately situated in the event of an air raid because of its height and slopes; the gases, which were heavier than air, would roll down the valleys. Lessons were learnt from a mock air raid on 3rd May 1939. By June 1939 seven wardens' posts had been established in Selsdon, and an auxiliary fire station set up in the hotel. However some kind of normality returned during the early months of 1940, and on 7th June 12 year old Pat Ford was crowned Selsdon May Queen in the garden of St. John's. Then the phoney war ended.

All leave for civil defence personnel was cancelled; plans were made to deal with cats, dogs and horses in air raids, suitable sites for allotments were sought and national savings groups were formed. Interestingly the Council would not let the LDV (forerunners of the Home Guard) dig trenches in the Recreation Ground.

From late September 1940 until April 1941 Selsdon had its share of the Blitz. Numerous bombs fell in the woods or on the golf course, but there was a number of incidents causing damage and fatalities. Two people were killed when 20 and 22 Littleheath Road were destroyed. Two oil bombs hit St John's Church and church hall one evening, but there were no casualties. The worst incident during this period was on 15th March 1941, when four high explosive bombs destroyed or damaged a number of houses in Queenhill and Byron Roads, killing five people including a deputy post warden, who happened to be walking by at the time. One bomb fell in the garden of 108 Foxearth Road, but the blast went upwards and little damage was done. Mrs. Cole raised pennies for the Spitfire Fund by taking advantage of people's curiosity to see the crater.

There were no further air raid incidents for nearly three years. At the end of 1941 the Home Guard was reorganised and the 59th Battalion (Addington) formed under Lt.-Col. H.E. Peirce; there were two companies, E and F in Selsdon, besides a mounted company on horseback. On one occasion a mortar, known as a Blacker Bombard, was being demonstrated in its headquarters in the old Selsdon Park farmhouse, when the instructor unwittingly inserted a live – rather than a dummy – fuse, resulting in a hole in the wall and injuries to himself. During the war there were frequent National Savings campaigns; in October 1941 Selsdon was asked to contribute £1500 to buy a Bren gun carrier, and as a way of saying 'thank you' one was borrowed to give rides to children up and down Addington Road on a Saturday morning.

A Bren gun carrier, which had seen service in Norway, giving rides to children in Addington Road, 29th November 1941.   Photograph courtesy of Mike Little.

After pressure from both the Government and the local residents, a British Restaurant, run by the Council, was opened on 9th September 1942 in the hall above Bailey's Garage. For lunch there was meat and vegetables for 9d and soup or sweet for 3d. However, it failed to pay its way despite an influx of local voluntary help, and it was closed down on Christmas Eve 1943. At the end of 1942 a wartime nursery for young children was erected on a bombed site in Byron Road, designed to cater for 57 children, and this continued until March 1947, when the houseowners were pressing for their houses to be rebuilt. The Council arranged a number of 'Holidays at Home' during the summers of 1942 and 1943, including film shows, children's entertainments, open air dancing and concert parties. Because they had time on their hands, the wardens and firewatchers organised a number of social and sporting events. The Selsdon Players reported early in 1944 that they had given 29 shows in two years at local aerodromes, gun sites and camps. In March 1943 the answer given to a question at a Brains Trust 'What is wanted most in Selsdon after the War?' was 'A Community Centre'. Selsdon Park Hotel remained open throughout the war, and raised money for various wartime charities by supper dances, golf and snooker tournaments. It is said King Haakon of Norway stayed there, and General de Gaulle lived in Arundel Avenue for a short period. There was one mystery – when a 35 year old local man was shot whilst playing golf on Croham Hurst, and died later from his wounds. The culprit was never discovered.

Bombing returned to Selsdon in 1944 – on 24th March there was a spectacular fire raid in the district, with 50 houses ablaze. An elderly couple were killed when two bombs fell in Sundale Avenue. Then on 15th June the first V1 or doodlebug fell on South Croydon. For the next five or six months life was severely disrupted and many events were cancelled. Although many flying bombs exploded around its borders, only two actually fell on Selsdon. One fell in Ingham Road, and at 5 p.m. on Friday 30th July, a V1, which had touched a barrage balloon wire demolished seven houses and seriously damaged 20 at the top end of Farley Road. There appear to have been no fatalities and surprisingly few injuries. By October social activities started again. The Home Guard companies were stood down and this was celebrated by march pasts and dinners. Luckily no V2 rockets hit Selsdon and by April 1945 the wardens' posts were no longer manned at night. In September the Residents' Association celebrated the end of the war with a 'Final Flare' in the Recreation Ground, with a bonfire, fireworks and floodlit dancing.

A major irritation of those years was the bus service provided by London Transport. Over 100 residents attended a meeting in May 1946, at which not only a LPTB official was present but also the Branch Convener of the busmen's union. The latter said the busmen always regarded Selsdon as 'The Holy City', as the passengers always considered themselves to be right. The Board man agreed that Selsdon deserved a better service, but explained that they had fewer buses than before the war, more children were going to secondary schools in Croydon and Old Coulsdon, and more women were working. That was before Croydon Corporation embarked upon their large housing estate at 'Heathfield', later known as Monk's Hill, which affected the capacity of the 64 bus route. 17 years after the initial call for it, the 234 bus was extended from Riddlesdown to Selsdon on 26th October 1949, so that at long last Selsdon had a direct bus service to Purley. It must also be remembered that during this time few people had cars and it wasn't until 1950 that the first complaints about car parking in Addington Road were registered.

" The 'Holy City' they call it : Looks more like Holy war to me !"

'Selsdon Smiles' started in January 1947 with a dig at the bus service. From *Selsdon Gazette* 1971

A HISTORY OF SANDERSTEAD

In December 1946 the first issue of a revived *Selsdon Gazette* appeared, edited by the Residents' Association, and which is still delivered monthly to all households in Selsdon. Looking at copies of the *Gazette* for this period it becomes very clear that there was a great deal of social activity. There were dances every week, run by the Dance 1941 Club or the Cotillon Club, or run to raise funds for the British Legion, the Boy Scouts or one of the several cricket and football teams. There was however only one place to hold a dance then, and that was in the Selsdon Hall above Bailey's Garage. In November 1947 two Surrey County Council officials were disconcerted to find a public hall above a garage, discovered that the hall had never been licensed, and closed it down forthwith. For some months no public activities took place there, but eventually a licence was obtained.

During the war civil defence people had set up social and sporting activities, and these continued under the Selsdon CD Association. Besides dances there was a Gramophone Society, two Youth Clubs, a Bridge Club and a flourishing Evening Institute in Selsdon School. The political parties were active – the Communist Party attracted small but vociferous numbers to its meetings, whilst on the 15th March 1948 a future Prime Minister, then Parliamentary Secretary to the Minister of Transport, James Callaghan, spoke at a Labour Party meeting. In February 1947 there was even a Carroll Levis Talent Hunt competition in the Hall.

The lack of a proper community centre had prompted the formation of the Selsdon Community Association in April 1948, although an informal organisation had been extant for some years. The aim was to press the local authority to find a site for a community centre, and the Association would raise funds towards the cost of the building – which presumably the Council would erect – and towards the cost of running it. The Selsdon Community Association started off very enthusiastically, with most associations and many individuals joining and raising money in various ways. Exhibitions were held – one for Arts and Crafts in conjunction with the Festival of Britain celebrations in 1951, and one for Natural and Applied Science in 1952. The Scouts and Guides produced two GuiScout Tattoos in the Recreation Ground at night, the second one being floodlit by the searchlights from a local TA Unit.

Selsdon never acquired its Community Centre. By 1954 plans had been agreed with the local authorities for a centre and library costing £14,754 on the site of the present car park, with the Community Association paying its share, one third, over 30 years. However, the Government was trying to cut down on local council spending and declined to loan any money at the time. The centre was added to the Surrey Development Plan, but the owner of the site objected and it was not until 1964 that new plans for a hall and library were produced by the U.D.C. The Association had hoped to have some say in the management of the hall, but these hopes were brusquely quashed by Croydon Council, who now took over and made it quite clear that it wanted no local involvement. The present Selsdon Hall was opened in October 1966, but because of high charges was initially little used by local organisations. The Community Association was wound up in 1974 and its funds of £729 distributed between member clubs and societies. The present Selsdon Library opened at the same time, having moved from 'Langley Oaks', which was pulled down and a residential home erected in its place.

Although few houses were destroyed during the war, many were damaged and the necessary repairs, some which needed a licence, took time. Building restrictions limited the number of new private houses that could be built, and almost the only new houses were the Council houses in Dulverton Road, which were started in 1948; a scheme to build similar properties in Ingham Road fell through. Some new shops were erected, notably Sainsbury's, which opened on 27th February 1950. This was the firm's first modernised post war store – the old open windows Sainsbury's had used hitherto were replaced with armoured plate glass and new colours were used inside. It also served as a testing ground for many new ideas incorporated in its first self-service store opened in London Road, Croydon, later in the year. In May 1949 the repairs to the bomb-damaged St. John's Church had been completed, and the church was reconsecrated by the Bishop of Croydon. Work then started on a new brick-built church hall, which was completed the following year, so that by 1950 there was a hall large enough for dances and for the Selsdon Players, the Croham Players and the St John's Dramatic Society to hold their plays, and for meetings. In 1948 a Selsdon Branch of the National Federation of Old Age Pensioners was inaugurated and two years later two branches of the Townswomen's Guild were formed. In the 1950s the

A HISTORY OF SELSDON

Triangle which comprised a number of mature trees, was cleared and the GPO politely told not to park its vans there, although earlier a proposal to set up a coffee stall on the Triangle was turned down.

In the last 40 years Selsdon's population has increased, mainly due to the building of three sizeable modern housing estates. Before these were built there had been some one-road developments such as Lynne Close (1958), Mountwood Close, and two – Greystones Close and Cowley Crescent – built when two nursery gardens closed. The first estate, developed by Wates, was linked to, although not directly communicating with, its adjacent major redevelopment of the old Surrey Garden Village Trust smallholdings at Forestdale. This estate, Ashen Vale, was commenced in 1966 on similar land.

Selsdon Vale had been developed in pre-war days as an extension of the SGVT scheme. The plots had not really been suitable for market gardening, and after the war a number of them became poultry farms and piggeries, one of which was the cause of complaints from residents. The Trust was wound up in 1969, and Wimpeys proposed the erection of a large estate of 600 or so houses. The plans were strongly objected to in Selsdon, partly because of the impact of more traffic on Old Farleigh Road. Nevertheless the proposals were agreed and work on the estate began in 1972.

Many of the houses in Kingswood Way had large gardens, and many owners were tempted to sell off parts for building. Many planning applications were opposed, but Prowtings came forward with a plan to build higher-priced houses in 1978, with a new road, Kersey Drive, which bisected Kingswood Way – part of which was cut off.

Although not strictly in Selsdon, an estate on former allotments, and at one time the suggested site for a new secondary school, was laid out at Ridge Langley in 1971. One small development did not succeed; a plan for some infill housing in Littleheath Road was vigorously opposed.

At this stage it should be noted that Selsdon returned to Croydon in 1965, when the new London Borough was inaugurated.

The parochial boundary of Selsdon had been extended to include Monk's Hill, and in December 1962 a new daughter church, St. Francis, was completed. Selsdon Baptist church was extended and rebuilt in 1957 and again recently extended. St. Columba's Roman Catholic church was rebuilt in 1962.

The 1950s and 1960s witnessed a great deal of discussion over the lack of provision of secondary education. The building of Riddlesdown School partly solved the problem and also later the opening of Monk's Hill School as it was then known relieved Selsdon Central School, which occupied the top floors of the present Selsdon School, closed in 1965. With the building of Selsdon Vale a new primary school, Greenvale, was opened in 1978. With the redevelopment of the centre of Croydon, the Girls' Public School Trust needed to find new premises for the High School, which was then in Wellesley Road. Land off Old Farleigh Road was purchased from the Hotel, and the new Croydon High School for Girls was completed in 1966, designed by Greenwood & Abercrombie.

Car parking became more of a problem in the 1960s, but the present car park was available from 1966, free until charges were introduced in 1997. Although traffic was increasing, it was not until 1968 that traffic lights were installed at the Addington Road/Farley Road junction. Despite regular complaints over the inadequacy or the infrequency of the services, the provision of public transport has improved in recent years. The 64 bus is still the main link with Croydon, although since 1997 it has been operated by Metrobus.

The Upper Selsdon Road route, once the 54, then the 12A, and latterly the 412, which also incorporates part of the 234 route, is serviced by South London Buses. Despite earlier requests to extend the bus service down Old Farleigh Road, it was not until the Selsdon Vale estate had been built that this occurred. Initially the young families who had moved there were against buses running through their estate. Indeed one man, who fortunately is still alive, threatened to lay in the road in front of the first bus to run through the estate. Metrobus persisted with its plans to run the 354 from Forestdale by way of Selsdon Vale and Old Farleigh Road to Croydon, and a frequent timetable now applies, with an hourly connection through the day to Bromley.

A successful innovation, begun in the late 1980s by Croydon Council, is the annual country fair held in Selsdon Woods in August each year. It is now a weekend event, and in recent years in fine weather it has attracted over 10,000 visitors.

Crime is not normally a major concern, but tragically in January 1982 a young woman was murdered in her bedroom in Foxearth Spur. Fortunately the perpetrator was caught and duly sentenced.

Selsdon Park Hotel remains a leading luxury hotel and conference centre on the outskirts of London, although the Sanderson family sold it to Principal Hotels in 1997. It did not obtain a full licence until 1970, in which year the Conservative shadow cabinet, in preparation for a forthcoming General Election, held a 15 hour policy discussion at the hotel. To quote Alan Sked and Chris Cook " it marked the beginning of the call to 'roll back the frontiers of government' and an end of liberal economics." It is possible that Harold Wilson may have coined, at the time of the Piltdown forgery exposure, the name 'Selsdon Man' for a mythical primitive beast destroying the benefits of Socialism in post-war Britain. For some months at least Selsdon came to the notice of the country.

It is unlikely that the real Selsdon Man was like that. Over the last 75 years Selsdon has changed, its social composition has altered and most of the houses are now at least 60 years old. There are still a few residents who have lived most of their lives in the same houses. The interiors have certainly altered; brick-built garages and fourth bedroom extensions added; double-glazed windows are almost universal and some newer roofs are evident, but the Costain house is still recognisable. Selsdon is now much greener again as street and garden trees have grown and matured and front garden fences have been removed or replaced by hedges and walls. Unfortunately today, most roads seem to have cars and vans permanently parked in them, or in the front gardens, which detracts somewhat from the original concept of 'a garden village'.

A Costain house in 1928.
Courtesy of Stan Cornish – he and his sister Joan are the two children.

Chapter 21

Chronology

by Joy Gadsby

c. 7000 BC	Mesolithic hunter-gatherers present using locally made flint tools.
c. 4500 BC	The first farmers began to till the soil.
c. 2000 BC	Bronze age – the first smiths arrived. A socketed bronze axe was lost or discarded in Sanderstead.
600BC - *c.*AD120	Iron-age farmsteads established in King's Wood and on the site now occupied by Atwood School.
c. AD 600	Anglo-Saxon cemetery in existence. It was discovered 7.3.1885 near Sanderstead Station.
c. AD 876-888	Aelderman Alfred bequeathed Sanderstead to his wife and children.
AD 964	Queen Ethelfleda, the first wife of King Edgar and mother of St. Edward, gave the Manor of Sanderstead to the new Minster at Winchester, later to become the Benedictine Abbey of Hyde.
1086	Sanderstead is recorded in Domesday Book.
1230	Building of Al Halon parish church began on an older foundation.
1250	Manor of Sanderstead leased to the Saunders family.
1272 & 1276	Boundary disputes between the Abbot of Hyde and the Prior of Bermondsey regarding Sanderstead and Warlingham.
1287	First mention of the sub-manor of Croham.
c.1310	Tower added to Al Halon Church; the wall paintings on each side of the east window probably painted about this time.
1324	Manor leased to the Bishop of Exeter.
1332	Tax assessment established the relative wealth of Sanderstead.
1489	Dedication of the parish church amended to All Saints'.
1530	Death of Dyones Atwood – her will confirmed the existence of St. Catherine's chapel within All Saints' church. Reference also to sheep farming locally.
1535	Henry VIII's *Valor Ecclesiasticus* includes the Rectory of Sanderstead.
1539	Manor of Sanderstead granted to Sir John Gresham.
1547	Sir John Gresham becomes Lord Mayor of London – one of several Sanderstead citizens to hold this office.
1575	Court case over grazing rights on Hamsey Heath.
1591	Transfer of the Manor of Sanderstead to John Ownstead – Serjeant of Her Majesty's carriage to Elizabeth I.
1600	Death of John Ownstead. Manor passed to his cousin, Harman Atwood. The Atwood family remained Lords of the Manor until 1919.
1653	Death of Harman Atwood. His fourth son, Harman Atwood II inherited the Manor.
1653-1658	Major Lewis Audley JP conducted marriages in his house at Purley Bury.

c. 6500 BC Britain became an island.

AD 43 Roman Emperor Claudius invades Britain.

1066 Battle of Hastings. William the Conqueror overthrows the Saxons.

1215 Magna Carta.

1348 Black Death decimates the population of England.

1539 Dissolution of the Monasteries by Henry VIII.

1588 Defeat of the Spanish Armada during the reign of Elizabeth I.

1603-1625 James I king.

1649-1660 Commonwealth under Oliver Cromwell.

1655	Mary, wife of Lewis Audley, died and was buried in Sanderstead church.	**1660** Restoration of Charles II.
1664	Hearth Tax levied on 11 houses in Sanderstead, including 'Sanderstead Court' and 'Purley Bury'.	**1665** The Great Plague.
1675	Almshouses at Warlingham built – for two residents from Warlingham, one from Chelsham and one from Sanderstead.	**1666** Fire of London.
1676	'Sanderstead Court' rebuilt by Harman Atwood – who died in the same year.	
1677	Henry Mellish, Merchant of the Levant, died of a 'wasting disease' contracted abroad.	**1678** Wool Tax imposed. Burial 'in wool' made law.
1693	George Mellish 'buried in velvet'.	
1710	Four knights of the shire, resident in Sanderstead, voted in the parliamentary election.	**1702-1714** Queen Anne.
1764	John Rocque's map of Surrey included a detailed survey of the lands in Sanderstead, showing fields already enclosed.	**1744** First coded cricket laws.
1770	Thomas Wigsell, a member of the Atwood family through the female line, inherited the Manor.	
1772	Baptism of Mr. St. John's slave in Sanderstead church.	
1798	Publication of T. Harding's *Twelve Hours Perambulation of the Rural Beauties of Sanderstead*.	**1776** American Declaration of Independence.
1802	The Parish Clerk, Robert Rutter, disappeared	
1805	– and is found drowned in a pond at Addington.	**1805** Battle of Trafalgar.
1809	George Smith, banker and director of the East India Company purchased Selsdon Park.	**1807** Abolition of slavery.
1813	Limpsfield Road Turnpike Trust established.	
1828 & 1832	Major repairs to Sanderstead Church undertaken. John Saker, bricklayer, signed a brick inlaid into the outer wall of the church.	
c. 1830	Sanderstead school opened in a cottage on Limpsfield Road.	
1841	Census mentions a village shop run by Eliza Nichols.	**1837** Accession of Queen Victoria.
1843	Tithe Apportionment Map drawn and the Sanderstead estate valued.	
1854	Benjamin Beeson survived the Charge of the Light Brigade at the Battle of Balaclava – and later became the village policeman.	**1847** Factory Act reduced daily working hours to 10 for women and children.
1870	The Manor woodland is converted to a game reserve and the gamekeeper's cottage built. First post box erected in Sanderstead.	**1870** Education Act - primary education for all.
1875	New school (now Gresham Junior School) built on land given by Colonel Wigsell. Croydon Rural Sanitary Authority set up. Houses condemned in Paddy's Bottom.	**1876** Telephone patented by Alexander Graham Bell.
1877-1890	Bishop of Rochester, Anthony Thorold, resident at Selsdon Park; ordained priests and deacons in All Saints' Church.	
1881	Two road casualties – Henry Hermitage and Willie Bex. Beginning of a Sanderstead Cricket Club.	
1884	Sanderstead Station opened on the London to Oxted line.	
1890	Sanderstead sub Post-Office opened in the Village Stores.	
1894	Establishment of Croydon Rural District Council which includes Sanderstead.	

CHRONOLOGY

1894	Sanderstead Parish Council established.
	Inauguration of Purley Downs Golf Course.
1894-1914	First phase of housing development in the north of the parish.
1899	Purley Oaks station opened on the London to Brighton line.
1901	Sanderstead Station parade of shops opened.
1903	St. Gertrude's RC Church opened.
1904	Sanderstead Lawn Tennis and Social Club founded.
	Poor Law Station established in Sanderstead. Samuel Cowdrey of 'The White House' appointed Assistant Overseer.
1907	Sanderstead Dramatic Club founded.
	First motor cars appeared on the roads in Sanderstead.
1908	Gas lighting introduced in Sanderstead.
	St. Mary's Church consecrated.
1909	St. Anne's College opened.
1915	Establishment of the Coulsdon and Purley Urban District Council – Sanderstead a constituent part.
1916	Captain Carpenter awarded the VC.
	Boy Scouts established for the first time. Girl Guides followed soon after.
1917	Sapper T. Holloway awarded the Military Medal.
1918	Corporal Basil Cowdrey awarded the Military Medal.
1919	Break-up of the Manor of Sanderstead – sold in two parts for development.
1921	First bus service commenced from Croydon to Sanderstead.
	First Sanderstead Branch of the Women's Institute formed.
1924	Borough Farm leased to David Bowerman, who began milk deliveries in Sanderstead.
1928	Shops opened by Purley Oaks station.
	De Havilland DH9 aircraft crashed in East Hill.
1929	Inauguration of Selsdon Park Golf Course.
c 1930	Electricity installed.
1931	Sanderstead Telephone Exchange opened with 814 subscribers.
1932	First shops opened in Cranleigh Parade.
1933	Hamsey Green parade of shops built.
	Congregational Church opened in Sanderstead Hill.
1934	Sanderstead Literary Society founded.
1935	Sanderstead Badminton Club founded.
1936	Sanderstead Fire Station built.
	All Saints' Church extension was built on north side including a chapel dedicated to St. Catherine.
1937	Boy Scouts and Girl Guides re-established.
1940	Dr Margaret Zeal was drowned while saving evacuee children.
1941	Sanderstead Horticultural Society founded during 'Dig for Victory' week.
	All Saints' Church roof severely damaged by incendiary bombs.
1942	Foundation of Sanderstead R.C. church – later to become the Church of the Holy Family.
1942	Sea Ranger Company SRS *Furious* established.

Side notes:

1901 Accession of Edward VII.

1910 Accession of George V
1914-18 World War I

1918 School leaving age raised to 14.
1919 Women aged 30 or over receive the vote.

1926 General Strike.

1936 Abdication of Edward VIII

1940/41 Battle of Britain.

A HISTORY OF SANDERSTEAD

1944	V1 landed in The Ridgeway causing fatalities and V2 landed in Purley Beeches, also causing fatalities.
1945	General rejoicing and improvised street parties to mark the surrender of Nazi Germany.
1949	Primary school opened in Tithepit Shaw Lane.
1950	Adult Education Centre opened in Sanderstead.
1952	Sanderstead & Selsdon Branch of the WEA began adult classes.
1954	Foundation stone of St. Edmund's Church, Riddlesdown, laid.
1955	Sanderstead Methodist Church founded.
	Ruth Ellis, wife of a Sanderstead dentist, was convicted of murder — the last female to be hanged in Britain.
1956	First branch of the Townswomen's Guild opened – at Riddlesdown.
1957	Foundation stone of St. Antony's Church, Hamsey Green, laid.
1958	Mitchley Hill Chapel opened.
	Riddlesdown High School opened.
	Ridgeway Infant and Junior School opened.
1960	Atwood Junior School opened.
1965	Sanderstead became part of the London Borough of Croydon.
	Tree Garden given by Eric Wettern to Croydon Council as a public open space.
1966	Coffee 'Roundabout' formed. (see page 122)
1967	The last steam train passed through Sanderstead Station.
1980	Sanderstead Parish church celebrates 750th anniversary by building St. Catherine's aisle.
1984	The children of Gresham Junior School began computer studies.
1987	Many trees lost in Sanderstead during the great storm.
1990	St. Anne's College closed – school amalgamates with Coloma School.
1993	Civil boundary changed at Hamsey Green – Sanderstead acquired a public house! (*The Good Companions* now inside the boundary).
1997	Formation of the Friends of King's Wood – to conserve the ancient woodland.

Side notes:

1953 Elizabeth II crowned.
1954 End of food rationing

1965 School leaving age raised to 16.

1971 Decimal coinage introduced.
1979 Margaret Thatcher first woman Prime Minister.

**Weathervane atop the wooden shingled spire of All Saints'
Church, Sanderstead.** *Photo courtesy of Stuart Pickford*

THE BOURNE SOCIETY

The Bourne Society was founded in 1956 and takes its name from the underground streams which follow the lines of the A22 and A23 roads, meeting in Purley to flow northwards and form the River Wandle, which flows into the Thames at Wandsworth.

The objects of the Society – England's largest local history society – are to extend the knowledge of local history in Caterham, Chaldon, Chelsham, Chipstead, Coulsdon, Farleigh, Godstone, Kenley, Purley, Sanderstead, Whyteleafe, Warlingham and Woldingham, and to ensure the preservation of records and objects of historical interest. The Society's Membership Secretary, Mrs. J. Emery, 118 Coulsdon Road, Coulsdon, Surrey CR5 2LB, will be happy to provide details of membership and subscription rates. The Society's telephone number is 01883 349287.

The Bourne Society is a registered charity, and as well as general work it has active special-interest groups in archaeology, industrial archaeology, landscape history, photography and pub history. Regular meetings, events and outings are arranged. A wide range of publications are produced, including a quarterly **Bulletin** and annual *Local History Records* which are sent free to members. For prices and current availability contact John Tyerman, Publications Co-ordinator, 60 Onslow Gardens, Sanderstead CR2 9AT, telephone 0181 657 1202.

Some recent publications —

Books:

Village History Series. Vol. 1–Purley, editor Andy Higham (1996); Vol. 2–Caterham, editor Gwyneth Fookes (1997); Vol. 3–Sanderstead, editor Joy Gadsby (1998); Vol. 4–Warlingham, editor Dorothy Tutt, in preparation for publication in 1999.

A Centenary History of the Chipstead Valley Railway (Tattenham Corner Branch Line, 1897-1997).

The Way We Were - A Bourne Society Book of Days by John D. Matthews.

Leaflets:

Getting to know our Downland Villages – No. 1. Sanderstead (1997); No. 2. Godstone (1998); No. 3. Caterham in preparation.

Postcards:

Ancient and modern views of places in the Bourne Society area are available from local stationers.